Deconverted

Deconverted

The Deconstruction and Dismantling of the Contemporary Church

JEFFERY CHILDRESS
with JOHN S. KNOX
Foreword Kenneth G. Warren

WIPF & STOCK · Eugene, Oregon

DECONVERTED
The Deconstruction and Dismantling of the Contemporary Church

Copyright © 2022 Jeffery Childress and John S. Knox. All rights reserved. Except for brief quotations in critical publications or reviews, no part of this book may be reproduced in any manner without prior written permission from the publisher. Write: Permissions, Wipf and Stock Publishers, 199 W. 8th Ave., Suite 3, Eugene, OR 97401.

Wipf & Stock
An Imprint of Wipf and Stock Publishers
199 W. 8th Ave., Suite 3
Eugene, OR 97401

www.wipfandstock.com

PAPERBACK ISBN: 978-1-6667-9083-2
HARDCOVER ISBN: 978-1-6667-9090-0
EBOOK ISBN: 978-1-6667-9091-7

MARCH 7, 2022 12:44 PM

This book is dedicated to Carol,
my wife of 30 years.
To this day,
I've never stopped trying to impress her.

If we remain silent,
in a society that has chosen utter rebellion against God,
we are showing not only utter disrespect for God and His truth,
but we are not showing love for individuals
who are being deceived into thinking that
following their own desires, that following their own lusts,
that giving in to the deception of society,
will lead them to life. Instead, it will lead them to destruction
and unhappiness and death.

—James White[1]

---

1. White, "Jesus Defines Marriage."

Contents

Preface | ix

Foreword by Kenneth G. Warren | xi

Acknowledgements | xv

1   Introduction | 1
2   The Epidemic of the Emptying Church | 4
3   The Investigation—Why Christians Deconvert | 21
4   The Diagnosis—A Theological Inoculation | 43
5   Learning for the Church—The Toughest Apologetic | 71
6   Conclusion | 101

Appendix A | 107

Bibliography | 111

Index | 119

Preface

CHRISTIANITY IS DISTINCT FROM any other world religion, philosophy, or ideology in how it explains universal origin, meaning, destiny, and morality. The Christian message is also unique in its promise of a personal and life-changing relationship with the Creator God. One can hardly deny the influence that the Christian faith has had on humanity over the past two thousand years. Regardless of Christianity's influential history, today there is a growing number of people who have shifted away from their commitment to the message and mission of Jesus Christ. Shockingly, many people have rescinded their beliefs in the faith and have renounced their once deeply held spiritual convictions. This situation exposes—not only the flaws in recognizing the roots of apostasy within the church—but it also raises concerns regarding the modern church's inability to effectively influence society and culture.

This book explores the phenomenon of people with roots in the Christian worldview who completely shift their ideology and radically transform their perspectives to the point where they now consider their previous beliefs to be evil and destructive. The impact of this wave of deconversion on the Christian church will be examined, as will the impact of the epidemic of postmodernism, cultural Marxism, and other ideologically relevant societal whims of America in the twenty-first century. The objective for this research was to identify why people would shift ideologies so radically without any supporting evidence, why the church is so

Preface

vulnerable to this phenomenon, and to determine for the church what apologetic or discipleship learnings and applications can be derived.

It is alarming that the modern Christian church seems so inadequate in its efforts to disciple and mentor those sitting in the pews today. Succinctly, this book investigates two main matters: 1) why the church becomes a victim of society instead of an influencer of society and 2) what can the faithful learn from those who have gone through this deconversion process. Apostasy, heresy, and rejection of the faith are nothing new in church history, but 2,000 years after the Christian movement began (and as the church moves closer and closer to the end times), it is important to educate and empower believers on how to witness and minister to a society hell-bent on abandoning God, Jesus, and the Way.

Foreword

IN THE PAST FIFTY years, our world has changed in dramatic ways—and so has the church of Jesus Christ in America. One such change within church life involves the changes in terminology due to the cultural shifts taking place in society. It was only ten-to-fifteen years ago that I first heard the term, *De-churched*, which is often used to identify those individuals who were once a part of a local body of believers but no longer have deep roots within the church. Those who have left church are on their own religious journey typically because they have been wounded by an individual in the church or were injured through their overall church experience. They are simply in great emotional pain but have not necessarily given up on God, completely.

The great thing about the *De-churched* is that some of these individuals may have continued to have a relationship with Christ and could be sitting on the back row of a local church on many particular Sunday mornings. Still, they typically do not want to be involved in the ministries of congregation and are content just to sit and soak it all in (rather than engage in the work of the Lord). Some of this may be understandable in the short-term, but it is detrimental for these individuals to remain in this setting for longer periods of time.

Another term that has been introduced within the church is a growing population of individuals who have been labeled "Nones."[1] As part of the downward spiral the church is now within,

---

1. White, *Rise of the Nones*.

FOREWORD

this growing population expresses no interest in the church or religion. Thankfully, there are a growing number of religious efforts that are being geared toward reaching the "Nones."

A third and newer term that is being used increasingly more in the last five years would be the term, "de-converted" or "de-conversion." This designation is used to describe those individuals who were living the Christian life (or at least living it in part through their words and actions). Yet, these individuals came to a point in their lives where they felt called to publicly denounce their faith. They no longer have any desire to follow the teachings of Christ, nor to honor the very God in whom they once placed their eternal hope. All the above represent different phases of belief that individuals find themselves in and represent very challenging issues that the church is also faced with in postmodernity.

Childress and Knox are correct in asserting that "De-conversion" has the potential to deconstruct and dismantle the contemporary church as we know it. In the last few years, society has witnessed the media explode with high-ranking church leaders, pastors, and prolific Christian authors and musicians leaving Christianity. The media loves to report these stories as if to say, "I told you so," or to promote the viewpoint, "that Christian stuff is nothing but a sham." In doing so, many of these individuals have abandoned the church with seemingly minimal remorse and have often apologized to general society in the form of a conflicted statement like, "I was wrong to believe what I was believing, but now I believe in what I am believing."

Clearly, the church is at a crossroads in many ways and will need to come to a better understanding of these new segments of people—some of whom have been engaged in the local church in the past. If the church fails to better understand these groups, then in a way, the church is contributing to its own demise, which should concern all who love the *Bride of Christ*. Confusion abounds when one who has claimed the name of Christ, only to years later denounce the name of Christ. Not surprisingly, such actions lead to feelings of frustration and hopelessness for many within the church.

Foreword

As such, the church must be armed with the knowledge to better understand the circumstances and internal impetus that is leading individuals away from the faith and toward a movement that leads these individuals to more disillusionment than what they already may be experiencing. The church must "step to the plate" and provide solutions for this sad and escalating anti-church, anti-God, and anti-Jesus movement. In 1 Peter 3:15 (NIV), Peter says, "But in your hearts revere Christ as Lord. Always be prepared to give an answer to everyone who asks you to give the reason for the hope that you have. But do this with gentleness and respect."

I am happy to report that Jeffery Childress and John Knox specifically and succinctly address such issues in their book, *Deconverted: The Deconstruction and Dismantling of the Contemporary Church*. The authors' passion for the church to be prepared to give an answer for the problem of de-conversion is palpable. Moreover, it is done in a way in which readers will be pointed to Christ and His truth as the answer, while being equipped to better share the hope of Christ with one who is possibly in the process of de-conversion.

This book is not about casting stones. Rather, at its core, it is focused on equipping the body of Christ with a greater knowledge of the "Why" behind someone who de-converts, the psychology behind the de-conversion process, and an overall high-level apologetic approach toward engaging with this evolving movement that is taking place in the postmodern church.

Believers should want to better understand this movement of the "De-converted" and I am convinced that Childress and Knox's book will benefit the church in an extraordinary way, through cultivating new avenues of ministry so that the church through Jesus can reverse the disturbing postmodern movement of "De-conversion." I am thrilled to endorse this book and believe that it will become a game-changer for those who are serious about seeing believers standing firm in the faith until the Lord Jesus Christ returns or we are called home beforehand.

Dr. Kenneth G. Warren, D.Min.
Online Psychology Instructor
Liberty University

Acknowledgements

I COULD NEVER BEGIN a list of acknowledgments without mentioning my Lord and Savior Jesus Christ. He chased me for thirty-five years and I finally surrendered (but that is a story for a later book).

Also, this book was only possible due the editing, proofing, and general mentoring of Dr. John S. Knox. Knox was the graduate school mentor for my master's degree at Liberty and I truly believe God placed him in my life—certainly due to his invaluable insight into sociology, theology, and scholarly writing, but apparently God also saw a lack of goofy humor in my life as well. Dr. Knox addressed all those voids in abundance. Special thanks to Dr. Kenny Warren from Liberty University's Online Psychology Faculty for reviewing the book and contributing his insight to the Foreword.

I am also grateful for Dr. Joe Brown, pastor of the Restoration Church of the Carolinas in Indian Land, North Carolina; Dr. Mike Whitson, pastor of Indian Trail Baptist Church in Indian Trail, North Carolina; and for Keith Freedman, frequent Knox book editor and racquetball partner in Nampa, Idaho for taking time from their important schedules to review this book and provide their testimonials.

Finally, I would like to thank Carol, my wife of thirty years, and my three daughters—Taylor, Haley, and Kylie—for their continued support through the writing of this book. Speaking of which, this is the first book of my career, but I am already working on book two. With all, I try to remember the Apostle Paul's exhortation: "And whatever you do in word or deed, do everything

Acknowledgements

in the name of the Lord Jesus, giving thanks through Him to God the Father" (Colossians 3:17, *New American Standard Bible*). May God continue to lead and bless those that follow Him.

1

Introduction

THE SEPARATION BETWEEN THE ideological extremes of Christianity and atheism is as wide as the boundaries of the known universe; however, it is not uncommon for people to make that monumental leap from one worldview to the other. The Christian who decides to rescind his religious faith and embrace atheism (the "deconverted" Christian, also known as an *apostate*[1]) initiates a wholesale reanalysis of the transcendent, of the self, of meaning, of morals, and of purpose.

Christianity is distinct from any other world religion, philosophy, or ideology in how it explains universal origin, meaning, destiny, and morality. The Christian message is also unique in its promise of a personal and life-changing relationship with the Creator God. One can hardly deny the influence that the Christian faith has had on global social existence over the past two thousand years. However, a growing number of believers who once claimed commitment to the transcendent message and transformative power of Jesus Christ have begun to rescind their belief in the faith

1. In theological literature, "Apostasy" is a common term to describe religious deconversion and is viewed as an act of opposition that entails making a statement against the exited group. In other words, an "Apostate" is someone who not only leaves the group, but who actively opposes it. The terms will be used interchangeably in this examination.

and renounce formerly deeply held spiritual convictions. This phenomenon concerning people with roots in the Christian worldview who completely shift their ideology, radically transforming their perspectives to the point where they now consider their previous system of belief as evil and destructive invites exploration.

Many people take other tracks post-deconversion, such a shift to other religions or even a move to what one may consider to be "passive Christianity," which involves a rejection of formal religious worship and community without necessarily rejecting the transcendent possibility of God or Jesus as an ideal example to humanity. Not surprisingly, postmodernity has shifted its focus and given approval to the apostate. The abyss between the two ideologies of belief and disbelief also correlates to the metaphorical gap between God and man—between a belief system based on a God-centered universe and a belief system based on a human-centered universe.

The recognition of a Creator-God has been a fundamental and ever-present tenet of humanity, embraced across many cultures and people groups. American philosopher and educator Mortimer Adler proclaimed, "More consequences for thought and action follow the affirmation or denial of God than from answering any other basic question."[2] Christianity, with its theological foundation being in the triune Godhead (which includes the person of Jesus Christ), started with a group of less than twenty people (probably uneducated laborers) and had its religious leader killed in a very public and embarrassing fashion at the hands of the Roman Empire.

Despite this improbable origin, which should have been catastrophic to any fledgling faith, it became the official religion of the entire Roman Empire within 300 years. Christianity is still the favored religion of one third of the world's population today. As of 2015, the United States has the largest population of Christians in the world.[3] However, since 1990, the percentage of the United States' population who consider themselves theists and followers

---

2. Adler, *Great Books*, 561.
3. Pew Research, "Countries With the 10 Largest Christian Populations."

INTRODUCTION

of Jesus Christ has reduced dramatically—along with a corresponding increase in the number of those who do not declare a religious ideological affiliation, also known as "Nones."[4]

This book seeks to investigate the rationale or apologetic behind the ideological shift away from belief in the Judeo-Christian God, the historically dominate influencer of Western culture and ethos. It will explore the possibility that society has a greater apologetic impact with anti-Christian principles than the church does in defense of Christian dogma. It will also explore the reality that people tend to intellectualize themselves away from the supernatural in favor of that which is natural, material, and therefore more "rational."

---

4. Pew Research, "In US, Decline of Christianity."

2

The Epidemic of the Emptying Church

THERE IS EVIDENCE OF a general shift in religiosity in the West. The impetus behind the shift is fodder for great sociological debate. Sociologist John S. Knox expounds on this topic in his work on radical individualism, which he termed, "Sacro-Egoism."[1] Knox illustrates the broad spectrum of thought in modern debate on the topic. He highlights the work of historian and sociologist Steve Bruce and his suggestion that even the modern religious have traded the transcendent for a version of naturalism.

What once was fundamental belief regarding the supernatural has "been diminished and is now psychologized or trivialized."[2] Bruce explains that religion heretofore was about the divine and our relationship thereto. The Bible is no longer seen as authoritative; Christ was merely a good teacher, miracles are unexplained phenomena, and God is a vague power and possibly—simply representative of our own consciousness. Ironically, many people who claim the aforementioned also still claim the label of "religious" or "spiritual." Some who hold those views also claim the

1. Knox, *Sacro-Egoism*.
2. Bruce, *God Is Dead*, 208.

label of "Christian" although those precepts have no basis in Jesus's teaching.

In what could be considered the capitalist perspective on religiosity, Knox highlights the work of Sociologists Roger Finke and Rodney Stark as they describe *rational choice theory*, suggesting that America is simply reacting to modern churches in a market economy perspective.[3] The churches who respond to the cultural shifts with the proper marketing will once again win their share of the market. Finke and Stark describe the conscious shift of the church as a lessening of "tension with the social environment."[4]

A variation in this theme is addressed in the work by British scholars Heelas and Woodhead in describing what they deem as the *Spiritual Revolution*.[5] Their research verifies evidence of this ideological shift. The authors state, "Some of the longitudinal data we have cited would appear to indicate that inner-life beliefs have overtaken or are overtaking beliefs more obviously belonging to a traditional theistic frame of reference."[6] They conclude that this shift may eventually completely replace the role once played by Christianity.[7]

In what will be a key theme of the apologetic response of this investigation, Hellas summarizes:

> (Modern) spirituality is experienced as dwelling within the here and now; as integral to life; as inseparable from, a natural aspect of, what it is to be alive. Rather than relying on external sources of significance or authority, considerable importance is attributed to the voice of experience; experience which emanates from the heart of one's subjective life, ultimately from one's life itself.[8]

Evidence suggests that there is a perception gap regarding one significant aspect of the human condition—personal

3. Stark and Finke, *Acts of Faith*.
4. Stark and Finke, *Acts of Faith*, 144.
5. Heelas et al., *The Spiritual Revolution*, 74.
6. Heelas et al., *The Spiritual Revolution*, 74.
7. Knox, *Sacro-Egoism*, 5.
8. Heelas, "The Infirmity Debate."

accountability. The deconverted Christians and current atheists who participated in this research regularly mentioned the "guilt" that Christianity added to their lives. Likewise, they claimed a release of the sense of guilt once deconverted, accompanied by a sense of overall "peace" (a word used quite regularly by the research participants), which described their post-deconversion mental state. They claimed a sense of conviction as a Christian and a sense of redemption as an atheist, which curiously, is completely reversed in the message of the Christian Gospel.

From a Judeo-Christian perspective, all people are born in sin and, therefore, have a fallen nature with tendencies toward evil versus good, but the same can be said of the naturalist characterization of humanity. In naturalism, humans are flawed creatures of a mindless process of evolution, who operate on the impulses of a hard-wired mental state, with a Darwinist focus on self-preservation. Concepts such as morality, purpose, and destiny are purely human constructs with no basis in physical reality, according to this worldview.

On the other hand, the message of Christ is that these qualities are indeed not only real and relevant, but in their objective basis lies the key to meaning and truth. Humanity has been provided an escape from its fallen state, an unearned gift of salvation and sanctification (John 8:24; John 14:6; Luke 5:23; Mark 16:6; John 3:16).[9] The atheist may not deny the utility of redemption, because they obviously continue to seek something similar, but they do debate where to source it.

Christianity declares a resolution to humanity's sins and guilt. However, despite the theology and message based on love, redemption, and victory, deconverted Christians claim an opposite experience. For these now avowed atheists, their religious experience carried with it a mountainous weight of guilt and judgement, expressions that are logical reactive implications to the theological term—sin.

---

[9]. Unless otherwise noted, all biblical references are from the N.A.S.B version. *New American Standard Bible* (LaHabra: The Lockman Foundation, 1995).

The word, "sin," occurs over four hundred times in the Bible. Sin is defined simply as disobedience to God. It can be considered a spiritual crime. The theological concepts of sin and redemption requires a constant evaluation of self. It requires a recognition of, and reckoning for, personal actions and accountability. It requires recognition of an objective standard of truth and the impact of deviation from that truth.

The theological mechanism for dealing with sin is acknowledgment, forgiveness, and repentance, concluding with reconciliation with God. One non-theological, twenty-first century, postmodern method of dealing with sin is to deny the concept even exists, believe that there is no objective truth, and then to deny any source of transcendent objective truth. Once that happens, the tension is relieved. It seems obvious that the Christian deconvert may have grappled with the formula of sin and redemption and eventually decided the weight of the struggle was too great.

Gresham Machen, in his great work, *Christianity and Liberalism*,[10] expounds on modern cultural rejection of fundamental Christian doctrines based on nothing more than a simple shift of presuppositions:

> Modern liberalism, it has been observed so far, has lost sight of two great presuppositions of the Christian message—the Living God and the fact of sin. The liberal doctrine of God and the liberal doctrine of man are both diametrically opposite to the Christian view. But the divergence concerns not only the presuppositions of the message, but also the message itself.[11]

Evidence from the research for this study suggests that those who struggle with their faith also struggle with the implications of moral auditing involving the de-emphasis of self, the conquering of the impact of sin in their lives and increasing personal introspection. Each of these are core aspects of the maturing believer in Christ. Atheism does not recognize supernatural authority nor

---

10. Machen, *Christianity and Liberalism*, 60.
11. Machen, *Christianity and Liberalism*, 69.

objective truth and as a result, seems attractive to someone struggling with purpose, meaning, and accountability.

Secular society is experiencing a similar shift regarding accountability. The political left propagates a worldview void of accountability—elimination of law and order by defunding institutions of safety, disregard for human life, societal change through intimidation, destruction, and rebellion, disassembling of the nuclear family, the installation of so-called "safe spaces" where students are isolated from intellectual challenges to their radical worldview, and even a challenge to the biological definition of a man or a woman.

Postmodernism is a twentieth-century philosophy characterized by skepticism, subjectivism, and relativism, suggesting a general suspicion of reason and ideology.[12] In essence, postmodernism rejects the prospect of truth and meaning in modern culture and society. While there is a clear drive for scientific improvement, environmental improvement, and a claim of political and social improvement, postmodern culture shows little evidence of a similar commitment for any concept of moral improvement. Stagnation seems to define morality for the postmodernist with the declaration, "You are good and acceptable the way you are right now."

The research from the interview participants for this project suggests deconverted Christians are not changing their religious perspective because of an evaluation of new and relevant evidence. Much like the postmodernist, they are shifting ideological perspectives seemingly as an escape, further validating the objective of postmodern thought in search for personal empowerment and more open social avenues. However, the exchange comes at a very significant price—both spiritually and psychologically, as will be examined later in this book.

Most of the former Christians who were interviewed for this research embraced key aspects of a secular worldview (even when they self-identified as a Christian believer), which aligned distinctly with American left of center politics. Since these leftist tenets conflict directly with historic Christian principles, this conflict of

12. Duignan, "Postmodernism."

ideology ultimately became intellectually unreconcilable, which instigated the deconversion decision.

In the first century, Jesus Christ also lived in an environment with true religious and political strife. He certainly could have chosen to leverage his influence among the Jewish proletariat (working class) to start a political rebellion against the Roman oppression. This was not the purpose or message of His mission. His message went beyond the natural, the material, or the political (Matthew 2:21). The singular mission of Jesus Christ was to influence humanity's recognition of objective morality and in doing so, all other aspects of the human condition would have the appropriate foundation to gain redemption, to become God-focused, and ultimately in following God's order for man, properly flourish.

For many in the political left in America, their intended scope of influence is not restricted to politics. The left has established a foothold or outright dominates many pillars of American society. The next target for the leftist agenda is the Christian church itself: they have directly in their sights the "religious left" due to the quite curious alignment of secular leftist social ideology with the religious left social sympathies.[13]

As an example, the twenty first century concept of "social justice," while promoters are happy to manipulate the Church with it when it suits their purpose, has its true origins in the secular ideologies of Karl Marx. This founder of Communism famously stated that religion is "at one and the same time, the expression of real suffering and a protest against real suffering. Religion is the sigh of the oppressed creature, the heart of a heartless world, and the soul of soul-less conditions. It is the opium of the people."[14] In his writings, Marx simultaneously mocks the basis of religion, but then admits it as a viable mechanism of manipulation that could be leveraged for his nefarious, social engineering purposes.

The twenty-first century concept of social justice is a not-so-subtle Marxist tool that perpetrates a continuous cycle of attack on institution and tradition, all while reinforcing the Communist

---

13. Bush, "Religious Liberals Want to Change."
14. O'Malley, *Critique of Hegel's Philosophy*, 4.

Manifesto narrative of the "oppressed" and the "oppressor."[15] It is being leveraged as a conduit to connect with socially ideological cousins; the political left and the religious left. Paul Kengor, political science professor expounds on this issue in his book, *The Devil and Karl Marx*.[16] Kengor suggests that although Western society has harshly judged socialism historically, he notes a recent and uncomfortable warming to the tenets of socialism. He explains, "The same softening on Marxism that has taken place in the realm of politics has also infected the church as well, at time through misunderstanding and at times through outright infiltration."[17]

While the political left ideologically identifies with tenets of Marxism, it takes a moral bridge to reach the religious left: enter the religion of Social Justice and its Marxist framework, critical race theory.[18] Pastor and author Dr. Tom Ascol shares concerns regarding the influence of the political left on the church and the potential impact to vulnerable Christians in a way that could encourage deconversion:

> The postmodern, deconstructionist worldview . . . has given rise to godless ideologies like radical feminism, Critical Race Theory, and Intersectionality," he wrote. "These ideologies are being smuggled into conservative Christian churches and entities (see Resolution 9 from SBC19) often by well-meaning but misguided teachers. If they are not identified and repudiated, they will have

---

15. Jost and Kay, "Social Justice," 1122–65.
16. Kengor, *The Devil and Karl Marx*, 5.
17. Kengor, *The Devil and Karl Marx*, 5.
18. Critical race theory (CRT), the view that the law and legal institutions are inherently racist and that race itself (instead of being biologically grounded and natural), is a socially constructed concept that is used by white people to further their economic and political interests at the expense of people of color. According to CRT, racial inequality emerges from the social, economic, and legal differences that white people create between "races" to maintain elite white interests in labor markets and politics, giving rise to poverty and criminality in many minority communities. The CRT movement officially organized itself in 1989, at the first annual Workshop on Critical Race Theory, though its intellectual origins date to the 1960s and '70s. See Curry, "Critical Race Theory," *Encyclopedia Britannica*.

disastrous consequences for the spread of the gospel and the faith of millions of people. These ideologies are not merely opposed but are actually antithetical to the gospel of Jesus Christ.[19]

The Neo-Marxist recognizes the absolute demonstrable failure of Marxism historically and attempts to resurrect the corpse with a much more attractive and embraceable facade. Neo-Marxism in America leverages concepts that are morally indisputable (such as the value of minority lives, the poor, and the disenfranchised), then inherently links those ideas to reprehensible, asinine, and thoroughly unbiblical ideas (such as redefinition of the nuclear family, the weaponization of race, the destruction of all foundations of tradition, including the church). However, specific to its utilitarian perspective of religion, Neo-Marxism does not want to rid Christianity of its influential substructure, but rather of its theistic and Christocentric bedrock.

The political left now dominates three major cultural pillars of American society including academia, entertainment media, and news media. Just as with Communism and Marxism, the church is yet another cultural landmark. Kengor expounds on this issue:

> Though it has been long obvious to sentient human beings that communists hate religion, they nevertheless had an almost preternatural ability to enchant liberal Christians. They cynically, contemptuously targeted the religious left. They knew that progressive Christians shared certain sympathies with them: worker's rights, wealth redistribution, shrinking the income gap, denouncing the rich, fomenting class envy. Communists exploited that trust, often invoking the language of "social justice" to enlist liberals in their petitions, their marches, their campaigns, their objectives.[20]

In strategically targeting the church, they seek to gain a new level of perceived legitimacy for their ideology to completely dominate culture. The church must be prepared to address the

---

19. Tolston, "Akin, Mohler Dispute Claim."
20. Kengor, *The Devil and Karl Marx*, 151.

onslaught of a progressive or postmodern push in American society and the acceptance of similar ideologies that lack any biblical basis or support among the church body.

In recognizing how to balance an accurate reflection of the true gospel of Jesus Christ with an awareness of the appropriate apologetic response to this spiritual warfare, the church can accomplish multiple things. Yet, the church must recognize this manipulation and improve their spiritual discernment regarding these tactics and their furtive and evil intention. It must be strategic and sensible in its efforts.

First, the Christian church can better understand what is meant by serving God with all our heart, soul, and mind (Mark 12:29–31) by sharpening apologetic tools to intellectually counter this twenty-first century culture wave. Second, believers can take an aggressive step in achieving the mandate of the Great Commission by understanding that the church must not be a bystander in the current culture war. As Machen states, "Light may at times be an impertinent intruder, but it is always beneficial in the end."[21] Third, believers can establish a beachfront counter the cultural propaganda by demonstrating that Christianity is the best possible explanation, the most complete holistic worldview, and the only viable framework to recognize objective morality and ethics on a global basis, across cultural boundaries—while at the same time showing that Jesus Christ has a unique and specific purpose for each person, individually.

Apologist William Lane Craig challenges the claim of some non-theists that objective moral values can and do exist in the absence of a Creator-God.[22] Craig is further astounded by such a claim given the questionable logic of Naturalism, the most popular form of atheism. Naturalism posits a claim that reality is defined only by natural properties and causes, as described by scientific method. Naturalists are amenable to some abstracts such as morality and moral realism. Craig points out that science is morally neutral. It may suggest evidence on the observable universe, but

---

21. Machen, *Christianity and Liberalism*, 1.
22. Craig, *On-Guard*, 131.

it is silent on questions such as moral obligations and duties. To suggest otherwise is simply to extend atheism and naturalism into a real of its own faith-based religion.

By understanding the motivation of the Christian deconverts, believers may find evidence to refine the Christian apologetic toward the whole of society. The apostate may be "Patient Zero" in a path to develop an apologetic inoculation against the disease of secular influence on the church. The medical community values the epidemiological investigations from the first reported case of a new disease. Epidemiologists trace these first patients (Patient Zero) to obtain clues about the infections transmission course and how to stop it spreading further.[23] This same strategy can be applied to spiritual plagues as well. In other words, an evaluation of the deconverted may inform the church of where our apologetical, doctrinal, and spiritual antibodies are insufficient barriers to the virus of postmodern ideology. The twenty-first century Christian apologist can (and should) learn from the personal experience of the deconverted.

Modern worldviews have an epistemology from one of three dimensions: the evidential (a thesis based on an evidence or "proof" basis), the experiential (a thesis based on personal experience as support for the embraced worldview), and the presuppositional (a thesis based on foundational knowledge which is presumed). The tendency to embrace a given dimension is impacted by societal norms and ideologies. Baby boomers have a stronger tendency toward presuppositions. Gen Xs have greater tendencies toward being evidentialist and pragmatic. Millennials and Gen Zs demonstrate a strong entrenchment in experientialism.

Given the reality of modern social norms and tendencies, people are fleeing the Christian faith due to various personal, social, and theological drivers. Even with these common ideological epistemologies, everyone has some degree of philosophical presuppositions. During the interviews for this book, the identification of newly discovered evidence was never offered as justification for the

---

23. Mohammadi, "Finding Patient Zero," 294.

dramatic worldview shift from Christianity to atheism. Rather, the shift occurred as a change of opinion on a single presupposition.

Every participant in this study personally decided that God was no longer a viable concept for them to recognize. For many, the transition was not immediate, but it was definitive. The evolution of their ideology was driven by experiences or questions that they could no longer reconcile, then later transitioned to a complete worldview shift on a cultural and philosophical basis.

Psychologist Karen Ross completed a similar study on deconversion for the University of Toronto. Ross similarly interviewed deconverts and her analysis concluded that the participants' ideological transition was characterized by emotional shifts (associated with a loss of loyalty to God) and intellectual shifts (associated with a loss of belief in God's existence), also with no mention of evidential discoveries in the process. Two typologies of experience emerged from the intellectual shift: one characterized by a sense of relief and the other by a sense of struggle.

Ross, in describing the phenomenology of deconversion, suggests a gradual cognitive evolution from an initial loss of faith (primarily associated with emotional shifts involving trust and loyalty to God). This emotional status is weakened by specific feelings of frustration, abandonment, disillusion, and apathy. Loss of faith then transposes to loss of belief (the state of being convinced of the reality of a phenomenon, such as God). The basis of belief is generally undermined by evaluation of evidence or further intellectual shifts.[24]

From this broader research on deconversion, it appears that atheists do reflect a tendency to be *community-seekers*. This definition of *community* could be interpreted internally (the fellowship with the like-minded) or externally (contributed involvement in support of those in need within their societal reach). Knox highlights this dynamic in his book, *Sacro-Egoism*, when a surveyed atheist referenced both aspects of the definition of community as an appealing aspect of Christian life.[25]

---

24. Ross, "Losing Faith," 120.
25. Knox, *Sacro-Egoism*, 116.

The modern atheist wants to protect their new lifestyle and find emotional support and safe harbor for their new ideology, so they create or join this artificial community of the like-minded. While this seems a relatively benign motivation, something else must be in play for the deconverted to go to an ideological extreme and now declare their once-embraced religious belief as being inherently evil. One must question if a person is dependent upon a community of the like-minded as intellectual or emotional reinforcement, and whether that reflects the depth—or the tenuousness—of one's commitment.

The research for this book suggests that the shift rarely has a basis in the evidential. Furthermore, the common responses from the survey participants suggest that society and cultural tenets carry a greater influence over personal ideology today than theological perspectives. Christianity is seen as closing social avenues due to outdated "fundamentalist" beliefs. There is a consistency among those surveyed that they had a foot in two quite different ideological camps—there was an attempt to balance socially and politically liberal personal preferences against a backdrop of an ideologically conservative (using modern precepts) biblical framework. In essence, their lives had become a living contradiction.

The survey participants offered explanations to the impetus to their deconversion that correspond in some respects with rational choice theory.[26] As a social construct, rational choice theory focus on self-interest seems untenable on a macro level. It seems unlikely an entire society could balance a drive toward a mutually beneficial purpose if the basis of every member's values was driven by personal priority and personal subjectivity. Rational choice theory (RTC) is the antithesis of the Judeo-Christian worldview because the top of the hierarchy of post-modern values espoused by RTC is indeed the self; the top of the Christian hierarchy of

---

26. Rational choice theory can apply to a variety of areas, including economics, psychology, philosophy, and recently, in theology. This theory states that individuals use their self-interests to make choices that will provide them with the greatest personal benefit.

values is God, which can secularly be posited as something beyond the self.

Judeo-Christianity is grounded on God and family; the latter extending to include community and country (Matthew 22:36-40). When those groups benefit collectively, the individuals benefit by default. It is not coincidental that most of those believers in the Judeo-Christian ethic also tend to lean conservatively as well. The political, social, and theological principles align. In the case of every one of the survey participants, there was misalignment across these same spectrums. This research suggests there is great learning for the church to effectively comprehend, confront, and combat this tension.

America's cultural past centered around faith. In the twenty-first century, it has shifted from a theological emphasis to a philosophical emphasis, heavily grounded in postmodernism. This shift may have caused an undesirable side-effect of confusion in the search for objective truth. The fact that America has lost its ability to effectively discern truth from ideological propaganda is not just a political problem or societal problem; it is a moral-centered, religious worldview problem. America has lost its objective ethical awareness. The fact that people are attempting to establish that compass, that sense of objective morality, on something political, societal, ideological—or anything other than theological—is an absolute testament to the postmodernist thinking that dominates today's culture.

Emile Cammaerts asserts, "When men choose not to believe in God, they do not thereafter believe in nothing. They become capable of believing in anything."[27] This is the challenge for Western society, for the church, and for the Christian apologist. A shift away from the theistic grounding in objective morality has, and will continue to be, the quintessential challenge of the twenty-first century and beyond. A rejection of objective truth raises the potential for an embrace of ideas that are destructive to the nuclear family, to a stable society, to a healthy worldwide economy, and to a God-centered worldview.

---

27. Cammaerts, *The Laughing Prophet*, 87.

This book suggests that there are opportunities for a successful apologetic strategy with the deconverted. It shows that those who have deconverted from Christianity have done so for reasons that are not insurmountable, whether intellectual, theological, or ideological. Furthermore, evidence has been provided as to how the church can identify potential deconverts and establish an improved discipleship strategy to address the personal and spiritual needs of those attacked by doubt and disappointment.

Western culture is experiencing a significant shift of thinking regarding the validity and utility of religious institutions, practices, and doctrine. Religious "Nones" (those who claim no religious belief or categorization) have increased from 8% in 1990 to over 20% by 2014 and continues to increase each year.[28] This shift aligns with the obvious influence of post-modern thinking on culture, given anti-theistic bias in media, higher education, and aggressive leftist agendas that challenge historically key western societal tenets, including objective morality, nationalism, capitalism, and religious institutions in general.

There is evidence, given the research for this book, reflecting a corollary between the political leanings of former Christians and the eventual declaration of insufficient theistic evidence. For example, all but one of the interview participants (93%) espoused politically left social views even as a Christian and did not shift their political views post-deconversion. The one exception to this was a conservative Christian and conservative voter who had a very negative experience with his church. Post-deconversion, he shifted his political leaning from conservative to liberal.[29] Identified by Knox as "Sacro-Egoists," this group is characterized by their beliefs that morality comes simply through a privatized sense of right and wrong.[30]

There is also biblical support to suggest that some people who "deconvert" were not actually committed Christians, regardless of the loose claim to the label. Jesus suggested there will be people

---

28. Pew Research, "Findings from the Religious Landscape."
29. Dagneau, "Deconversion and Liberal Theology."
30. Knox, *Sacro-Egoism*, 16.

with a flawed perspective of what being a Christian authentically entails. He stated, "Not everyone who says to me, 'Lord, Lord,' will enter the kingdom of heaven, but the one who has done the will of my Father who is in heaven" (Matthew 7:21). Christianity is a life commitment, not a membership of a la carte moral choices (I John 4:20; John 8:12; Luke 9:62).

Approximately half of the participants in this research responded with tepid support of fundamental biblical principles regarding marriage, family, and objective truth. It would be legitimate to question whether these individuals were truly converted believers, whether they had a truly accurate intellectual understanding of Christian principles, whether they truly had a life-focused commitment, and whether they were on a devoted spiritual journey of growth and maturation in the faith. However, most of the participants did indeed self-describe as having an intellectually engaged, life-centered commitment to Christian principles espoused in Holy Scripture.

As a result, the Christian apologist seems to have multiple ideological challenges in attempting to address the deconverted, but all the challenges still have a common denominator—that being, a worldview that rejects the fact that morality has an objective, transcendent basis.

Given the decreasing influence of Baby Boomers (born 1946–1964) and Gen X (born 1964–1979) on the current culture, churches seem to have established a push toward the dimension of experientialism embraced by Millennials and Gen Z (born 1980–current). The spiritually transcendent seems to have been exchanged for the emotional, the social, and the proximate. Prayer time has been exchanged for interpretive dance and skit presentations. Doctrinal preaching has been replaced by a type of religion that is Christ-less (too controversial) and non-biblical (too much conflict with popular [or vulgar] culture). It seems appropriate to ask again the question that theologian Dietrich Bonhoeffer famously asked as he explored this phenomenon after the turn of the twentieth century, "Who is Christ for us today?"[31]

---

31. Westhuizen, "'Who is Christ?,'" 143–67.

The Epidemic of the Emptying Church

As a result, Christian churches are losing their ability to distinguish themselves from culture. There is no reason to see church as the only source of truth when one can saturate themselves with personal affirmation with modern philosophy on countless blogs and YouTube videos. The church, with its perceived outdated morality, outdated source of truth, lack of commitment from its own congregants, and its inability to compete with liberal propaganda, is outgunned, outmanned, and societally ineffectual. As a result, the Christian message—through a compromised church—has become irrelevant. One could only imagine the letter that the Apostle Paul would write to the twenty-first century Christian church.

The Christian church has been doctrinally crippled with large percentages of current congregants believing that eternal salvation can be obtained through "doing good" and embracing the belief that having "some kind of faith" is better than having a particular kind of faith. These claims are not defended by historical Christianity, nor are they defended by biblical scripture.[32] If the church itself is veering away from core elements of the Christian faith, what hope is there in the ability for religious institutions to provide effective discipleship for those who are already spiritually vulnerable and weakly grounded in truth? Christian leaders must embrace one monumental reality; the next wave of apostates is sitting in the pews of the modern church today.

The research for this book, which focuses on personal interviews with Christian deconverts who now self-categorized as atheists[33] (as well as existing qualitative scholarly research on the subject), asserts that the deconverts tend to fall into three categories as drivers of their deconversion: 1) negative personal experiences with religious institutions, 2) personal experiences that "disproved" the probable existence of God, and 3) moral concerns with Christian dogma and doctrine.

Regardless of the preferred label of "Agnostic" (unknowingness) by most the interview participants, there was a posture of outright rejection of God's existence among interview participants

---

32. Showalter, "US Christians Increasing Departing."
33. Pew Research, "Countries With the 10 Largest Christian."

as opposed to a claim of not being convinced that God does not exist—the former, traditionally a descriptor of atheism rather than agnosticism. As a result of the personal, subjective nature of the reasons that stimulated the deconversion process and the lack of positive evidence for disbelief in God, this book suggests that an appropriate apologetic strategy can be established for this group. In other words, the research uncovered no evidence to suggest a closed door in the mind of the self-proclaimed Christian deconvert. To the church, this should provide clear motivation that this is still a legitimate mission field.

3

The Investigation—
Why Christians Deconvert

A THOROUGH ANALYSIS OF the participant responses reflected several common themes. While the individual stories varied, each person provided similar conclusions that drove a re-evaluation of their belief system. Surprisingly, the deconverted Christian can be viewed as a more extreme version of a "seeker"—a term that typically has a religious aspirant connotation.

While one can conclude this ideological shift was to initially to reject their previous faith, the deconverted ultimately sought something to replace the void. This results assessment will focus on two key areas: the rise of naturalism as an apparent intellectually defensible alternative to Christianity and the theological vulnerability of the modern Christian as a result of a weak apologetic training. There was a clear delineation of the basis for deconversion between two areas: intellectual or emotional reasons for deconversion. The research participants offered no positive proofs of atheism that prompted their ideological shift. All the evidence offered represented proof of a conclusion that Christianity was void of legitimacy. This section will also highlight the most common objections to Christianity identified from the interviews.

Another significant conclusion is that this research should be instructive, if not an outright warning, to the church. The pews of the modern church should be the priority mission field for Christian apologist. The greatest challenge to the twenty-first century church does not come from outside the church, but from within. The modern Christian is ill-prepared for the level of spiritual and cultural warfare being waged against them today. Today's Christian church seems to lack a proper theological grounding (or embraces an abandonment) for topics such as objective morality, biblical authority, and other fundamentals of Christian apologetics.

Additionally, the analysis of this research underscores the need for Christians to seek out deconverted Christians and build a bridge—not simply offer a soundbite apologetic. The self-avowed atheist will benefit most by seeing the Christian testimony as an expression of a person's life, not just by wise and crafty argument.

As Chesterton remarks,

> It is no good to tell an atheist that he is an atheist; or to charge a denier of immortality with the infamy of denying it; or to imagine that one can force an opponent to admit he is wrong, by proving that he is wrong on somebody else's principles, but not on his own. After the great example of St. Thomas, the principle stands, or ought always to have stood established; that we must either not argue with a man at all, or we must argue on his grounds and not ours.[1]

This observation raises an additional learning for the apologist: one must be prepared to go into the territory of their interlocutor, just as the Apostle Paul did with the Greeks (Acts 17:22–31).

One issue was abundantly clear from the interviews—not only had the former Christians ultimately decided to switch their most fundamental worldview presupposition from assuming the existence of God to denying the existence of God, but they were also quite emotional about it. Some were resentful; some were downright angry. Christianity was positioned among the group of brainwashing ideologies that feeds off the vulnerable. This cynical

---

1. Chesterton, *St. Thomas Aquinas*, 49.

perspective certainly presents a unique apologetic challenge due to the fact these individuals already had an experience with Christianity and explicitly rejected it.

It was intuitive, since their new ideology had a basis only in what is natural and material, that the deconvert would have identified newfound evidence against a Creator-Deity, or against biblical prophecy, or against the resurrection of Jesus, or any other major points of Christian doctrine. This is not the case. From comments in the interviews, it was apparent that these beliefs were simply brushed away, without newfound evidence, as being fantastical faith-claims of the delusional. However, in not a single conversation among the research participants was new evidence provided to defend the radical shift in worldview. This represents an additional apologetic challenge; belief in Christianity was replaced with a worldview void of positive support and fortified by a strong base of resentment and anger toward Christianity and religion in general.

This raises the most troubling question from this research; what could prompt someone to completely shift the fundamental basis of their view of the universe, life, morality, and truth without any evidence to support their new ideological basis? Certainly, the argument of an inability to prove a negative could be claimed here, but these people, whom the majority claimed that their Christian belief was indeed intellectually grounded at the time, now make a 180-degree claim; that being, that Christians are willing victims of religious propaganda and manufactured, wide-scale delusion. This perspective will be evaluated further in the Apologetic Response section of this book as a primary motivator to their deconversion and a fatal defeater to their Christian ideology.

In evaluating many of the interview participants' self-assessments of their understanding of Christian doctrine and principles, it would be easy to make an a priori claim that their belief was based on flawed doctrinal interpretation. In that case, these deconverts were not truly followers of Christ and historic Christianity, but rather flawed, mutant ideologues. In this case, the religious apostate is simply falling victim to the influence of post-modern society and the New Atheism is battling against a strawman version of the Christian Gospel.

Among all the hours of interviews, not a single comment was presented as serious response to a "steelman interpretation"[2] of the Gospel—only comments of distortion and caricature, such as their claims of the Bible's support for chattel slavery or their claims of biblical support for rape victims to marry their attacker (more details of interview responses are included in the Results and Response Assessment section of this book). It was evident that the choice was not easy for most of them.

The interview participants frequently cited damaged friend and family relationships resulting from their decision. They fully committed to the choice and their 180-degree worldview shift pivoted upon that decision. When asked to self-identify to three definitions of atheistic unbelief,[3] most respondents self-identified as agnostic; yet, when pressed as to the depths of their convictions on the subject, the answers more clearly fit into the more traditional atheist or even anti-theist worldview (sometimes called "subversive"[4]) versus the more benign category of agnostic.

The research suggests some commonality regarding demographics, societal predilections, and political archetypes among the research group. All were now members of an organized atheist organization. All, with one exception, were Caucasian. All, with one exception (Mormon), were previously from predominantly evangelical, Protestant denominations. The vast majority considered themselves politically left-of-center, even when they were

---

2. A philosophical positioning of an argument to give it proper rationale and justification. A steelman is the antithesis of a "strawman" tactic that would strive to weaken an argument so as to make it easier to defeat.

3. Three definitions of atheistic worldview were provided to the interviewees; 1) atheism—one who does not believe in God and the issue is resolved in my mind, 2) agnosticism—one who does not have any evidence for or against God, but I am open to where the evidence leads, and 3) anti-theism—one who openly declares belief in atheism as well as believe that religion is itself evil. See Cragun and Hammer, "One Person's Apostate is Another Person's Convert," 149–75.

4. Bromley, *The Politics of Religious Apostasy*, 5.

THE INVESTIGATION—WHY CHRISTIANS DECONVERT

Christians. Once deconverted, all espoused left of center politics, even the few who previously held to politically conservative principles. All had subtle variations in their definition of atheism. About half considered their religious views to be "life-centered" and "fully intellectually embraced." The other half clearly did not espouse common fundamental biblical principles and their general embrace of Christianity was more through family influence versus intellectual commitment.

All except one of the interviewed deconverts now reject any claim in support of the transcendent. The person who still recognized the possibility of transcendence embraced a concept of "spirituality," which was based on a sort of Darwinian and universally shared empowerment, although no source for such a "power" was offered in evidence. Most now considered all religions to be flawed ideologically, tools of abuse, a mechanism of brainwashing, and an absolute danger to society. About half noted that they missed the comradery, community, and relationship aspect of organized religion, suggesting that they have not found an equivalent since deconversion, even among the atheist community.

Most said they could not foresee anything that would convince them to embrace Christianity again. Some suggested that they miss the sense of purpose and meaning from the Christian philosophy. One person admitted that they now fear death more than before in daily living.

PSYCHOLOGICAL BASIS FOR DECONVERSION

Cognitive dissonance theory (CDT) describes the condition that when individuals hold two or more cognitions that are contradictory, they feel an unpleasant state—dissonance—until they can resolve this state by altering their cognitions.[5] Per Amanda Hinojosa and her Howard University team of contributors on the topic of CDT:

---

5. Adam, "Leaving the Fold," 42–63.

This uncomfortable state motivates individuals to seek a way to reduce the magnitude of dissonance experienced as a result of these discrepant cognitions. Hence, individuals can reduce dissonance by engaging in *discrepancy reduction*, which entails altering cognitions to reduce the cognitive discrepancy. Furthermore, individuals who are motivated by the negative affective state of dissonance to engage in discrepancy reduction can reduce dissonance by changing the original cognitions, adding/subtracting cognitions (e.g., new attitudes, behaviors, or beliefs), or adjusting the importance of the cognitions.[6]

An example cited by Hinojosa is the concept of intense socialization (e.g., hazing) by organizations. Typically, more common in an aggressive version with college fraternities and sororities. A softer version exists within corporate environments. The research supporting CDT shows that people will change their opinions and commitment about unpleasant tasks, if proper compensation and motivation is provided and reinforced, as this increased commitment justifies the unpleasant aspect of organizational tasks or concepts.

As this concept applies to religious apostates, note that most of the participants in this research maintained social or political perspectives that differed from common interpretations of biblical mandates identified with Christian doctrine. All except one of the interview participants (93%) declared a liberally political lean, even as a Christian. The search for discrepancy reduction was instigated by these participants and the search ended in an ultimate rejection of Christian belief. It appears that the process of cognitive balancing between culture and religious tradition may have significance in predicting potential loss of Christian faith.

Regarding such cognitive tensions, for example, while the Bible clearly prioritizes the value of life (Jeremiah 1:5; Exodus 20:13; Deuteronomy 5:17; Matthew 5:21–22), most study participants voted with the political left to support abortion. While the Bible clearly defines marriage as a holy covenant between one man and

---

6. Hinojosa et al., "Cognitive Dissonance Theory," 170–99.

one woman (Genesis 2:24; Malachi 2:14; Matthew 19:5–6), most supported leftist politics regarding homosexuality. While the priorities of Jesus and his apostles were clearly moral versus societal (Matthew 22:21: Romans 13:1), most of the research participants were supporters of modern concepts of so-called "social justice,"— a concept which has a thin, propagandized layer of legitimacy and righteousness, but in reality, has unrealistic and untenable societal "solutions" that are inherently based on Marxist principles of class hatred, political bias, destruction of national identity, and separatism.[7]

Oppression, in a modern society like the United States, is born, matured, and cultivated primarily as a social construct. Modern Western culture broadly sympathizes with the underdog and the less fortunate, and as a result, propaganda suggesting the existence of political oppression in the United States, although a purely Neo-Marxist social narrative, can be used as an amazingly effective tool to influence the ill-informed, for both the supposed oppressed as well as the supposed oppressor. The propagation of a false societal reality can be an effective tool in manipulating and giving voice not only to the legitimately disadvantaged, but also for leftists who want to hijack economic structures that cannot guarantee equality of outcome as the basis for nefarious social changes.[8]

Most people certainly desire "equality of opportunity;" that is, the basis of capitalism and the basis of the United States Constitution. The left wants to push the historically proven nonviability of the utopia of "equality of outcome;" this is the basis of historical and Neo-Marxism, Socialism, and Communism. Ultimately, counterfeit oppression can be used as a tool of oppression itself— a reality that has been exploited by social justice warriors, class warfare extremists, and purveyors of identity politics, even though the data suggests causation for the lineage of poverty and lack of

---

7. White, "To Black Lives Matter," 88–94.
8. D'Souza, *The Big Lie*, 129–34.

achievement in some communities which differs from the narrative of the Neo-Marxists.[9]

Economist and social theorist Thomas Sowell offers evidence to suggest the cause of the destruction of black culture in America is not the ubiquitous, yet unproven claim of systemic racism and white privilege, but rather the welfare state itself. Sowell emphasizes that there are two key failures in the dissemination of this propaganda. First, it points blame in the wrong place and secondly, in doing so, it distracts from drawing attention to legitimate issues affecting minorities. "You cannot take any people, of any color, and exempt them from the requirements of civilization—including work, behavioral standards, personal responsibility and all the other basic things that the clever intelligentsia disdain—without ruinous consequences to them and to society at large."[10]

This book draws specific attention to this issue for one significant reason: just as the claims of Neo-Marxism finds purchase in the minds of the disadvantaged themselves, it also finds fertile ground in the minds of socially liberal Christians. The church must recognize this fact and make it clear that that twenty-first century Christians can reach consensus on the existence of a problem without being bound to the foolish "solutions," which are being touted by peddlers of ideologies who not only do further harm to its constituents but are also blatantly opposite the tenets of Christian doctrine.[11]

While one could claim that the research population for this book is too modest to draw macro level conclusions about Christian deconversion, the findings correlate with research of larger scale, including professional psychological research on this topic. Per George Spyropoulos and his work on the psychological profile of deconversion at the University of Surrey: "Results reveal that participants relinquished deeply held religious beliefs after experiencing insurmountable tension on an emotional, cognitive and

---

9. Sowell, "Blame the Welfare State, not Racism."
10. Sowell, "Blame the Welfare State, not Racism."
11. D'Souza, *The Big Lie*, 202.

social level, which eventually led them to adopt a new identity of unbelief."[12]

On the surface, CDT appears counterintuitive to Christian deconversion. The influencing authority in this case is the church, which would be the corporate source of cognitive support, even in lieu of internal personal conflict with certain doctrines (e.g., dissonance). However, this scenario appears to be playing out in reverse. Given that the interview participants ultimately rejected their previous Christian beliefs, they ultimately granted cognitive authority to society and culture over Christianity. Once this dissonance was resolved in their minds, all other elements of the Christian cognitive framework tumbled like a house of cards; God, Jesus, the Bible, the resurrection, and Christian authority suddenly were bankrupt concepts.[13]

A summarization of the post-deconversion religious perspectives of the participants and their comments reveal a radical shift of presuppositions. There was complete consensus among the apostates that the Bible is not authoritative; on the contrary, it is harmful. Specific comments included, "The Bible clearly supports rape" (referencing Deuteronomy 22:23–29 as proof), "Christian apologists struggle to defend the Bible's clear support of slavery" (referencing Exodus 21:1; Ephesians 6:5; 1 Timothy 6:5), and "The Bible is full of contradictions and errors."

One self-declared anti-theist remarked, "I don't see parallel in what is described in the Bible compared to reality in the world today. Every religion makes same claims; prayers being answered; so-called miracles, and so on. There is confirmation bias in the interpretation of certain events purely with an objective to manipulate the masses."

Finally, a former church group leader noted,

> Once you stop looking at the Bible as not a holy book, but as a book, it just falls apart at that point. I am a bit embarrassed that I believed it so long. I lived my whole life following what I now believe is a lie. I now have

12. Spyropoulos, "A Portfolio of Academic, Therapeutic Practice."
13. Lee and Gubi, "Breaking Up with Jesus," 171–84.

freedom in my current belief. Science is more satisfying than anything I felt religiously. I believe people who [are Christians] have blinders on. [Devotion to scientific fact] changed everything about my worldview.

As one would expect, the apostate's perspective of the Divine changed radically as well, claiming no evidence of a *good* God. Comments included, "How can a *good* God allow evil?" from a man who lost his job due to mental health considerations, "How could God, if he existed, allow me to lose my career?" and from a committed anti-theist, "If God exists as described in the Bible, he is not worthy of worship."

Furthermore, while few self-categorized as anti-theists, their angry comments certainly reflected evidence as such. With one exception, all the participants stated that religion is an evil influence on society. Comments included, "The majority of my atheist friends are more loving than Christians. Organized religion is just rigid; an organization devoted to indoctrination. People should think for themselves. Even Christian children are more judgmental than non-Christians. It is based on a philosophy of shame and repression. For example, why is organized religion so controlling of sexuality?" The former church leader concluded, "Religion is a blight on the world. Most of the world is suffering. Stupidity is a result of religion, and the world would be a better place without it. Even if it is proven beyond a shadow of doubt that God exists, I would not worship him."

Participants were asked to provide a numerical range for their depth of belief during the time that they were a self-professed Christian. The categories of belief reflected elements of both core Christian creeds as well as secondary doctrinal issues. The score range was 1 (disagree) to 5 (strongly agree). A score of 3 would reflect "no opinion." The highest average scores, reflecting strongest depth of belief, were regarding 1) the claim that there is a personal Creator-God, 2) that Jesus Christ was bodily resurrected, and 3) that prayer is an effective tool of faith. This perspective on prayer is contradictory, given the low percentage of time that liberal Christians spend in prayer.

The Investigation — Why Christians Deconvert

The lowest rated questions, reflecting weak or non-existent agreement with doctrine even while they were self-professed Christians, involved 1) homosexuality being defined as a sin in the Bible, 2) evidence of cosmology, archeology, or objective morality as proof of God, and 3) the Bible being inerrant and relevant in all its teachings and truth. It is notable how closely these sentiments also generally align with liberal Christian churches. This peculiar ideological alignment will be explored further in the Apologetics section later in this book.

The obvious question must be posed regarding this effort to resolve cognitive dissonance between liberal social tenets and Christian principles—why is the church losing its authoritative role, even amongst professing Christians? There was no new evidence that drove the shift; it was simply a change of personal perspective on Theism. The apologetic learning is that the church should not just establish *what* the Christian presuppositions are and *what* the biblical principles are, but *why*. The church must provide a more appropriate grounding on how biblical truths impact individuals, culture, society and why these factors should be considered amongst the theological presuppositions.

God's truth has deep, life-changing implications for humanity. The modern Christian is apparently not adequately equipped with a proper understanding of the psychological utility of God's moral directives. Theistic authority and the implied authority of Scripture has been lost in translation, certainly amongst the white noise of subjective postmodern cultural babble.[14] Notable to the research was the fact that while the deconversion represented a galactic shift of their religious, spiritual, moral perspective, for all participants save one, it did not cause any deviation in their social and political perspectives.

Most already maintained left of center social and political perspectives, even though they realized many of the ideas they embraced conflicted with the teachings of the Bible. This conflict was rationalized as evidence of the Bible being "written for an ancient culture" with "no reflective of advanced cultural perspectives." This

---

14. Streib et al., "Deconversion," 41.

view of a foundational element of Christian truth will be evaluated later as a second fatal exposure to apostasy.

The challenge to evangelize those who have not experienced or recognize the transcendent is not simple or straightforward. However, to establish an apologetic for those who *have* had that personal experience, who once claimed to be a follower of Jesus, who actively embraced a Christian worldview, and who once shared in a commitment to a higher power is a particularly daunting apologetic challenge. Improper or ineffective biblical teaching and weak or non-existence presuppositional defense seems to debilitate the intellectual, certainly the theological, foundational support for the Christian worldview, ultimately leading to a rejection of Christian belief.

Christians tend to reference personal experience of the supernatural as demonstrating the "hard" evidence for the existence of God. However, as a stand-alone apologetic, the ability to move from evidence to proof for this claim falls short in the eyes of the skeptic. As a result, believers are in a continual battle of "the most plausible explanation" in defense of the Christian worldview, certainly as is the case for the atheist, although the skeptic tends never to offer tangible evidence to support their anti-theistic claims.

Even more surprising is the fact that virtually every deconvert, given their new presupposition, now proclaimed religion itself as destructive. Terms such as "brainwashing," "indoctrination," and "evil" were used as descriptors of the institution of religion. While most participants somewhat reluctantly considered their past Christian exposure as contributing to a more rounded personal life experience, many stated that they regretted their time as a believer.

Modern atheists generally seem to apply a unique strategy to counter the concept of a Creator God. First, there is a collective rejection based on insufficient evidence ("I don't see enough evidence for a god"). As a something of a fallback plan, the second tactic is a rejection of the morals of the Christian God, even if He does exist ("I wouldn't worship such an evil, sexist, racist, homophobic god"). The third tactic, as an extension of the claim of an "immoral" God, is to challenge the God-centered structure and framework of the universe itself.

This third premise is based on a deistic ad homonym claim that God (again, as a fallback claim, even if He exists) is playing an evil "game" with humanity. God is a nasty kid with a magnifying glass, and we are the ants.[15] The accusation from the apostate is that God sets up the game of life as a ruse, a spoof, or a con, primarily for our ultimate failure. In doing so, God is reflecting His true nature; instead of being loving and good as portrayed in the Bible, He is, in reality, immoral and unjust. It is a game of deception, of bait and switch, and ultimately of pure wanton, indiscriminate evil. In essence, if God exists, His grand intention is to simply play an evil game with humanity. So, they say.

In summarizing comments from the apostates into a formal declaration, the following is a summation of the atheist's "God's Evil Game" rules. First, establish *perfection* (Eden), then give God's fallible creations the ability to corrupt perfection, simply through the so-called "gift" of free-will (the transcendent equivalent of "bait and switch"). God made humans fallible, then blames them for their fallibility. Second, because of the gift of free-will, God established an ultimate penalty for the wrong choice in exercising that so-called gift. Furthermore, He established death as the ultimate penalty for even the innocent descendants of those who exercised that gift. Therefore, the so-called gift actually is a death sentence—not of culpability, but simply of heredity.

Third, allow for pain, suffering, injustice, heartache, moral evil, natural evil, and dispair to exist, even for those who believe in God, despite the religious propaganda that he or she is a "loving God." Allow just enough of a veil to exist on the question of the transcendent and the supernatural so that there will never be absolute proof, only arguable evidence, which must be aggressively learned, shared, and defended; inspired and reinforced only by blind trust and wishful thinking.

Also, hold all of humanity accountable, despite their inferior intellect and limited knowledge (which God designed), to pass

15. Dueck, "Angry at the God."

the impossible test between the choice of unobservable theistic transcendence verses observable, material, reality. Finally, allow natural evils to exist (hurricanes, floods, disease, and so on), which cause devastation on believer and unbeliever alike, good and bad people alike, productive and non-productive alike—although a "good God" could easily stop those things from happening. "God's Evil Game" bonus points: relegate those that make the choice against worshiping God to a permanent, eternal penalty, even if they live otherwise moral and virtuous lives.

The net impact of the trilateral argument is the ultimate intellectual "get out of jail free card" for non-theists to escape any burden of proof in the debate. Either God is playing the game because He is immoral, or religion is playing the game because, in reality, a god is not there. The final conclusion, given the irrationality of the God Game, is that God is simply a Christian-based, deluded fantasy or that religion is simply a tool for manipulation of the masses.

Regardless of the level of vitriol of the modern atheist, a primary quest by humanity throughout history has been to seek proof of, and communion with, the Creator God. A primary question by postmodernists in the twenty-first century is why would a god play these sorts of games with his creation? To the atheist, it is not logical or reasonable and therefore, fails the test of the cynic and the skeptic, or in the minds of the apostate, it fails even the test of morality. The atheist fails to consider the possibility that God would test the heart of human beings; primarily for purposes of stimulating more openness to His presence, secondarily for purposes of personal maturation and deeper moral introspection.

Atheism, given its basis of naturalism, posits the claim against Christianity as being simply a manmade construct. Yet, the replacement ideology is certainly a manmade creation—that being, secular humanism and its ideological cousins. Atheists reject one form of worship and replace it with another—one based unapologetically on human reasoning, naturalism, and the worship of self.

Based on the current cultural debate on objective truth and morality, from a theological perspective, one could make a claim that all ideologies eventually boil down to two options. While many denominations and philosophical varieties are claimed, the debate seems to center around two base ideologies with a supreme entity at the top of each hierarchy of values:

1) God is God.
2) The individual is God.

Graham Oppy explains this worldview dichotomy from a secular perspective: "Big pictures divide into two parts: that which is common to a range of competing big pictures, which I call data, and that which is distinctive of particular big pictures, which I call worldview. So, for a given atheistic big picture and theistic big picture, what they agree on is data, and what they disagree on is, respectively, atheistic worldview and theistic worldview."[16] As a result, the choice is simple, yet profound. Humanity's perspective of reality is influenced by a fundamental choice: either God is truly God, or in the alternative, man sits alone at the top of his own hierarchy of values.

The hierarchy of values embraced by the atheist has a curiously dualistic framework. God is judged as unjust because of the biblical tenet that death is consequence of sin and evil. However, the atheist and their ideological cousins support the freedom for women to choose to kill the unborn—not based on medical criteria, but simply based on the prerogative of choice. God is judged as a homophobe and Christians are judged as "anti-science" when the Bible establishes the union of a man and woman as the ideal framework for family and children, even though ample scientific studies prove the social, intellectual, and emotional benefit during a child's developmental years of having a simultaneous male and female parental influence in the home.[17]

Given the responses from the research participants, the atheist decries the objective moral accountability of theism and attempt to establish subjective morality as a viable alternative. Some take an entirely different tactic and suggest that morality is nothing more than a human construct that places an unfair and

16. Oppy, *Atheism*, 177.
17. Milkie, "Changes in the Cultural Model," 223–53.

unnecessary burden on people who should instead be affirmed as "fine the way they are." Societally, subjective morality is untenable and worse, stagnant morality is self-defeating.

For society to benefit, moral evaluation, maturation, and growth must be embraced once again as a tenet of strength and stability. Former Attorney General William Barr expounded on this issue in a 2019 speech at Notre Dame on the topic of religious liberty. Barr explained how the early founders of the American Constitution initiated a great experiment in balancing the limit of coercive powers of the government with trust in the self-discipline and virtue of the American people—a trust in the ability for each person to have the capacity to restrain and govern themselves.

In essence, the societal embrace of the concept of objective morality was expected:

> But what was the source of this internal controlling power? In a free republic, those restraints could not be handed down from above by philosopher kings. Instead, social order must flow up from the people themselves -- freely obeying the dictates of inwardly possessed and commonly shared moral values. And to control willful human beings, with an infinite capacity to rationalize, those moral values must rest on authority independent of men's wills -- they must flow from the transcendent Supreme Being.[18]

The Christian church must become more effective in leading people to this truth. Morality originates from an objective basis. Without reconciling this fact, Western society will continue to wonder in an ethical desert, so thirsty for anything that resembles truth that they are willing to drink the sand.

EMOTIONAL BASIS FOR DECONVERSION

The second category of impetus for deconversion included those who had personal experiences that challenged their ideological

---

18. Barr, "Address on Religious Liberty."

The Investigation—Why Christians Deconvert

foundations regarding the transcendent, in general. This subset of research participants specifically concluded that they were so angry with God for allowing certain experiences in their life, that the experience itself proved God cannot exist. Even as the stories were deeply moving, the circular reasoning cannot be ignored.

Carl is a thirty-something who was raised in a Christian home although he had never completely embraced fundamental Christian doctrine.[19] He told the story of being forced out of his chosen profession, one which he was deeply passionate, due to complications from his bipolar disorder diagnosis. Carl admitted respect for his parents and their deep Christian roots, but he eventually decided to break from their ideological perspectives. In essence, Carl could not reconcile that God allowed him to be removed from a career where he had such a deeply rooted passion. As a result, he concluded there must not be a real, personal, transcendent, deity. Carl lamented, "If one existed, how could God have allowed this horrible chain of events to occur?"

John is a fifty-year-old, former active Southern Baptist congregant. While he self-assessed with the deepest level of conviction about core Christian doctrine (the existence of a personal God, Jesus's resurrection, the inerrancy of the Bible, and so on), John admitted to doubts. During the interview, he shared the deeply personal and moving story of his twenty-year-old son committing suicide. In the months following this tragedy, not a single person from the church (including the Pastor) reached out to minister to John and his family. John had always seen the Christian community as an important facet of his family's life; however, when he needed support the most, there was none. John's deconversion had a monumental impact on his worldview and ideology and included a political shift from right-wing conservative to liberalism.

In both situations, the deconverts had life experiences where they perceived God's hiddenness at a point when He was needed

---

19. All names have been changed to protect actual identity. Demographic information regarding the interviewees is reflective of the interviewee's own self-assessment.

the most. Their final analysis was decidedly Epicurean: God was not capable, not caring, or simply not there at all.

Another common thread among the interviewees was the perceived failing of Christianity to withstand intellectual, moral, philosophical, and/or historical vetting. Most had embraced secular humanism or other closely related non-theistic ideology. One exception was a woman who embraced spirituality but rejected the concept of a personal deity. Even after two and a half hours with this person, no evidence was provided to support a claim of "spirituality" void of a theistic basis.

Most of these individuals seemed particularly angry with religion in general, to the point where many were quite comfortable to self-describe as "anti-theists;" the belief that religion is not just a benign ideology, but a dangerous one. While the participants tended to be quite aggressive with their claims against the Christian worldview, yet again, no evidence was provided against the existence of God. Rather, the majority claimed that God had not made Himself sufficiently visible in their lives.

Modern atheists tend to draw a mocking parallel to belief in God as an equivalent belief in Santa Clause, the Tooth Fairy, or the flying spaghetti monster.[20] Yet, even amongst the religious, the concept of moral therapeutic deism exists.[21] To wit, for believers, a personal God should also be a personal protector from all things negative, painful, or distressing. He is the great affirmer and deflector. However, Scripture clearly refutes this concept (John 16:33, Matthew 16:24, John 15:20).

In defense of the atheist (and the immature Christian as well), this frustration regarding prayer and the apparent hiddenness of God is understandable if one views the process as a "spiritualized Amazon dot com" where one places the orders and God provisions—with expedited shipping. To the unbeliever, if God fails to deliver the expected product or service in the expected amount of time, then simply move on to the next deity. The God-concept to

20. Dawkins, *The God Delusion*, 53.
21. Smith, *Soul Searching*, 163.

the spiritually immature is a consumer-driven perspective of the Divine.

C. S. Lewis, who in his atheist years wrote under the pseudonym of Clive Hamilton, voiced this perspective of God's apparent hiddenness prior to his spiritual conversion: "The trouble with God is that he is like a person who never acknowledges one's letters and so, in time, one comes to the conclusion that either that he does not exist or that you have got the wrong address."[22]

There are multiple parallels to the atheistic perspective of the world with the biblical story of the rich young ruler (Matthew 19:16–30; Mark 10: 17–31; Luke 18:18–30). A rich young man (likely a young leader in the local synagogue) approaches Jesus and asked what he could do to earn his way to heaven. Jesus replied in such a way as to distinguish the action of good deeds from the attitude of Christian obedience. The young man pressed Jesus further, stating that he had religiously kept all the commandments, but regardless of doing so, he sensed a gap. Jesus then commanded him to sell all his belongings and give the money to the poor. This obviously went beyond what the young man wanted to do, and he walked away, grieving.

At first glance, one could easily interpret Jesus's comments as simply providing more good deeds for the ruler to follow to earn his way to salvation (i.e., giving all his money to the poor), but this was not the crux of the lesson. Some scholars translate this passage as demonstrating supererogatory ethics (doing more than duty requires). This also misses the point of his teaching.

This passage is about faith and obedience, not earned redemption. Author and biblical scholar Warren Wiersbe highlights the good intentions of the young ruler in coming to Jesus with an open mind and an intention to learn.[23] The young man knew he had rigidly kept the commandments (as a good Jewish leader would be expected), but something was missing in his life. In a discussion regarding salvation, one must understand why Jesus would raise the issue of the Mosaic Law. Christ was not suggesting the law and

---

22. C. S. Lewis, *Spirits in Bondage*, 15.
23. Wiersby, *Bible Exposition Commentary*, 72.

righteousness were the route to salvation, but that this failure of conscience was evidence that humanity *needs* salvation. Wiersby emphasizes, "The law is a mirror that reveals what we are."[24]

Furthermore, Christ suggested that the young man give all his wealth to the poor, not as a supererogatory act of earning redemption, but as a demonstration that redemption was truly through faith—and the greatest demonstration of faith is through Christian obedience. First-century Greek traditions reported that aristocratic young men who wanted to study under famous teachers also tended to be too spoiled to submit to what their teachers demanded.[25] Christ sensed the same with this young man. Wealth was not his sin; the fact that religiosity and wealth had become his god was his downfall.

The same can be said of modern culture. From the interviews, the Christian deconverts seem to take this much further. They expected God to work on their schedule and on their priorities. God, in essence, had to earn their respect and if He did not, they rejected Him (see a biblical example of this in Job 2:10). God is not expecting someone to earn His favor—and He certainly is not attempting to earn humanity's favor. Truth matters more than propaganda. A Christian is one who has devoted his life to Christ and displays that devotion in obedience; any other variation of this truth is a humanist creation of a different, self-centered, false religion.

What sits atop a person's hierarchy of values, what a person spends the most time thinking about, what is of most value to an individual; that is a person's deity. Jesus taught this lesson to the young ruler (Matthew 19:16–22). A person cannot earn his way to heaven. It is a door that is opened by faith, trust, sacrifice, and obedience to Christ, above all else.

Apostates seem to experience the same sense of wanting. They attempt to fill that undeniable, subconscious longing for redemption with good deeds. Atheist organizations tend to have strategies for strong community outreach programs. The former

---

24. Wiersby, *Bible Exposition Commentary*, 73.
25. Keener, *Bible Background Commentary*, 94.

The Investigation—Why Christians Deconvert

Christians certainly did not understand the lesson of the rich young ruler when they were believers—and they attempt to seek fulfillment down a similarly flawed and empty path.

Somewhat surprisingly and without exception, the former believers described the decision to renounce Christianity as a decision that was followed by an overwhelming sense of peace. As stated by Carl (the gentleman who suffered from bipolar disorder and lost the opportunity to pursue his chosen career):

> Why would God allow this to happen to me? It took me years to reconcile this. Maybe there was not meaning to it. Maybe there was not a God to make it happen. As I said this to myself, things suddenly started to make sense. It was peaceful. The alternative was that there was someone all powerful, who loved me and was letting this happen to me. If nobody was there (on a transcendent level), then there was no reason to be mad.

Joanna, a former Mormon, had similar sentiments:

> The feeling of constant judgmentalism, the conditional love, the earned righteousness; all was overwhelming. In essence, your value is conditioned on your actions. Once that was eliminated from my life, I felt an overwhelming sense of peace that I did not need to carry that burden anymore.

Another participant reflected on a very different basis for deconversion, albeit with the same result:

> Cosmology was huge thing for me. When you begin to look at the Bible not as a holy book but as any other book, it just falls apart at that point. I'm a bit embarrassed that I believed it so long. I lived my whole life holding to something that I now believe is a lie. There is freedom with atheism. Science and rationality are more satisfying than anything I felt religiously. I believe Christians have blinders on. My deconversion changed everything about my worldview.

Ironically, when asked about what they missed most about the Christian experience, as well as what they feared in life today, many responses seemed to counter the previous claim of newfound peace. Multiple participants lamented the loss of community that they experienced as a Christian. One regretted the loss of assurance of an eternal life. In a very intense moment with one participant, she mentioned that she now fears death more than ever before.

One may conclude that the there was a trade-off occurring in the deconversion. Removing God as righteous judge and the objective basis of morality also relives them of personal accountability. The apostate now seeks a replacement source of comfort—one that can provide that same vestige of freedom with a corresponding sense of meaning, hope, and purpose with the appearance of righteousness.

4

The Diagnosis—
A Theological Inoculation

THIS SECTION WILL DISCUSS the appropriate apologetic response to the challenge posed by the modern deconverted Christian. The church has numerous challenges to address that will not be included in the scope of this book (i.e., rampant accusations of sexual misconduct, poor leadership oversight of financials and staff accountability, and embarrassing moral failures of clergy and other church leaders) but will instead focus on the obligation of the church to proclaim the Gospel of Jesus Christ and build disciples with deep roots intellectually, philosophically, and theologically via a strong apologetic focus.

It would seem logical that the evidential support for Christ's resurrection would be the central attack target of the apostate, since that single point, if determined to be false, defeats the entire framework of Christian belief. Curiously, none of the interviewees suggested that the historical Christ was a primary factor in rejecting the Christian faith. The deciding factor in deconversion was a shift in the presupposition about the existence of God.

While the deconverts proclaimed as strong a commitment to their new ideology as they once claimed with Christianity, the former Christians lacked an apologetic in defense of a societal benefit for the atheist worldview, other than the elimination of the evil of religion. The truth claims of the atheist worldview that highlight not only lack cohesion but demonstrate an outright contradiction.

One interesting aspect of the research for this book is the appearance—in virtually every aspect—of how modern atheism functions as religion, in its own right. The atheist community tends to favor the label, "freethinkers;" however, if humanity is nothing more than "slaves dancing to the tune of our DNA," evidence in support of the claim of free thinking lacks substantiation. Atheists proclaim lack of evidence in support of God; however, they offer no evidence to the contrary, suggesting they have no burden of proof on the matter—a claim some consider as intellectually lazy. Furthermore, the atheist does not just claim lack of recognition of God. They despise the idea of God, and they certainly loathe the Christian God.

Regardless, atheism unashamedly steals from the Christian worldview. The atheist postulates an idea of secular morality and yet, they can only posit clearly subjective opinions about morals based on a popular premise of human flourishing propagandized by the New Atheists. Atheist philosopher and author John Gray challenges each of these claims. Regarding his rejection of the propagandized labels of atheists (such as the title of freethinkers), Gray argues:

> While atheists call themselves freethinkers, for many today, atheism is a closed system of thought. That may be its chief attraction. When you explore older atheisms, you will find that some of your firmest convictions—secular or religious—are highly questionable. If this disturbs you, what you may be looking for is freedom from thinking. But if you are ready to leave behind the needs and hopes that many atheists have carried over from monotheism, you may find a burden has been lifted from you. Some older atheisms are oppressive and claustrophobic, like much of atheism at present time.[1]

---

1. Gray, *Seven Types of Atheism*, 2.

The Diagnosis—A Theological Inoculation

Regarding the angry and aggressive anti-theism from the so-called New Atheists, Gray confronts the alternative worldview promoted by the ideology:

> The new atheists have directed their campaign against a narrow segment of religion while failing to understand even that small part. Seeing religion as a system of beliefs, they have attacked it as if it was no more than an obsolete scientific theory. Hence, the "God-debate"—a tedious rerun of a Victorian squabble between science and religion. But the idea that religion consists of a bunch of discredited theories is itself a discredited theory—a relic of the nineteenth-century philosophy of Positivism.[2]

Criticism is not just coming from scholarly sources. There is growing popular challenge as well—not necessarily against the theistic arguments, but against the cultural milieu of hyper-skepticism. Humanist journalist Staks Rosch writes in the Huffington Post about this phenomenon and describes how he considers it to be psychologically detrimental to modern atheists:

> Atheists are notorious for being contrarians and for people who are not always joiners. You get three atheists in a room together and it will not be long before some minor issue divides them. SouthPark famously satirized this and in the past few years, we have seen this at our local and national meetings and events. But the fact is that if religion has done anything right, it has been to form actual communities for people to gather and share their struggles.[3]

There are two challenges presented. Even if one simply chooses to discard their presupposition about God without corresponding evidence, one must decide how to establish an objective standard for humanity in the absence of a transcendent moral code. A subjective basis of moral values and duties based on the imagined collective agreement of purpose and meaning seems

---

2. Gray, *Seven Types of Atheism*, 9.
3. Staks Roche, "Atheism has a Suicide Problem."

untenable, since culture cannot even establish such abstracts successfully on a secular micro level, not to mention a macro level.

Even families disagree on interpretations of culture, obviously as an extension of generational perspectives. How, therefore, could a similar moral code be stablished across vast generational and cultural boundaries for all of humanity, unless it is established in the moral framework which all of us have written imprinted in our conscience, that being, the moral framework of God? "They show the work of the law written in their hearts" (Romans 2:12–16, NASB).

Many prolific, yet less-prominent atheists, disagree with this philosophical sleight-of-hand by the new wave of anti-theists. Clinical evidence highlights the negative psychological impact of the atheist worldview. Not only do those who uphold religious beliefs hold statistically proven positive perspectives of life, the opposite is the case with non-believers. A 2004 study published in the *American Journal of Psychiatry* found that religiously unaffiliated subjects had significantly more lifetime suicide attempts and more first-degree relatives who committed suicide than subjects who endorsed a religious affiliation. Furthermore, subjects with no religious affiliation perceived fewer reasons for living and had fewer moral objections to suicide.[4]

In the study, religiously unaffiliated subjects had more lifetime impulsivity, aggression, and past substance abuse. No differences in the level of subjective and objective depression, hopelessness, or stressful life events were found. Religious affiliation is associated with less suicidal behavior, even among clinically depressed patients. Religiously unaffiliated subjects were younger, less often married, less often had children, and had less contact with family members. After other factors were controlled, it was found that greater moral objections to suicide and lower aggression level in religiously affiliated subjects may function as protective factors against suicide attempts.

From a secular perspective, author and clinical psychologist Jordan Peterson describes the concepts of "assimilation and

---

4. Dervic et al., "Religious Affiliation," 2303–08.

The Diagnosis—A Theological Inoculation

accommodation," posited by French child psychologist Jean Piaget, as drivers of humanity's search for cognitive balance and a sense of meaning.[5] In essence, a person must go beyond what he *has* become to what he *could* become. There are two ways of addressing the gap; assimilation (using an existing schema to deal with a new situation) or accommodation (when the existing schema does not work and needs to be changed to deal with a new situation). Using this language, Christian deconverts are experiencing psychological accommodation. They are retreating from their previously held beliefs in search of new beliefs that provide less dissonance (in other words, offering more "rational" alignment) regarding their status (current version) of themselves.

Per Peterson, the problem with the modern cultural and political ideologues is that they identify most with what they already are, instead of being able to "die" to their old dead structures (self) for something better to come forward. On a theological level, this directly correlates to man's redemption through Christ's death and His representation as the Logos.[6] However, for some, it seems that the status quo of self may be more desirable than personal and moral growth, despite the obvious psychological, intellectual, and emotional stagnation which may result.

If the apple tree could talk, it would scream out against the pruning saw. "This is painful! This is unfair! This is unnecessary! I was producing apples just fine!" The Christian recognizes that the benefit of the pruning process is greater than any temporary pain that may come from the process of self-analysis, in search of a better, more effective, self. A pruned tree is more healthy, more efficient, and more productive over time. A pruned character has more maturity, more resilience, better judgement, more stability, and is closer to the Logos.

The deconverted seems to define peace as retirement from the pursuit of what they *can* become; they fall back into the seemingly comforting embrace of the status quo. Their peace seems to

---

5. Peterson, "Piaget Segueing into Jung."

6. In Christology, the Logos (Greek: "Word," "Discourse," or "Reason") is a name or title of Jesus Christ, referenced in the prologue to the Gospel of John.

arise from bailing from the apparent strain of moral introspection. This logically aligns with the perspective of the political left as well. Acceptance of what a person is now is premium. Applied to the Christian church today, if one is a Christian with politically leftist beliefs, the reality of cognitive dissonance should be a warning; they are one presupposition away from ideological synchronization with the worldview of the devout atheist.

Christian church leadership must find a path to rebuild that bridge with current apostates as well as the future apostates that sit in their pews today, but they must do so by leveraging the unchanging truth of the Gospel of Jesus Christ. A watered-down Gospel will create watered-down converts with a truckload of cognitive dissonance in tow. Ravenhill proclaims steadfastly, "This generation of preachers is responsible for this generation of sinners."[7]

The apostate may express and justify their accommodation—their solution to spiritual cognitive dissonance—in many ways. In what may be the toughest apologetic, the twenty-first century apologist must be aware of these ideological offramps and be prepared to address them, albeit with truth and not cheap propaganda. The latter may work for the intellectually and morally vulnerable today, but it is not the appropriate vehicle for the Gospel (2 Timothy 4:2).

Regardless, it is important to note a difference between the post-deconverted seeker and the post-deconverted reprobate mind. The skeptic who now has committed his life to being an enemy of God should not deter our commitment to truth. There are people who have become enemies of God in an aggressive, frontal assault on Jesus Christ and His church. The church must know the difference and must not wilt to this assault. Their strategy includes outright political objectives of the elimination of constitutional protection of free speech and freedom of religion. However, for the average atheist, their ideological perspectives are more personal.

They question, challenge, deflect, and reject in a manner common for the average skeptic. The church has no need to consider these people as enemies of God. They rely on age-old claims, antiquated one-liners, and cascaded talking points of the non-theist

---

7. Ravenhill, *Why Revival Tarries*, 112.

The Diagnosis—A Theological Inoculation

community. Clay Jones explains the proper attitude of the Christian apologist in dealing with the average atheist or agnostic:

> That the skeptic might reply, "I wouldn't worship a God like that" matters not. Our goal is to present a theodicy that is biblically based and coherent. If we succeed in that, the fact that the skeptic doesn't like our answer is irrelevant. We are not trying to defend a god that the skeptic would worship. After all, a god that the skeptic would worship doesn't exist.[8]

Therefore, it is vitally important to identify those vulnerable in the church today. Once the mind is closed, it becomes exceedingly difficult to re-engage. The priority apologetic mission field for the modern church starts at the first seat in the first pew in church today.

DECONVERSION AND NATURALISM

Most of the deconverted Christians claimed to now embrace variations of naturalism,[9] including secular humanism, scientific naturalism, and moral naturalism. If naturalism is true, the human intellect is biologically pre-programmed. Naturalism suggests the universe was created by chance and arose out of chaos and everything in it functions as a normal course of natural law. Our thoughts are simple chemical reactions in the brain. Everything one thinks emerges from a background cause of which we have no control.[10] In essence, humans are simply DNA-driven robots. A person does not consciously make choices; their chemical reactions establish those as "choices" in their brain. Individuals are simply passive observers.

The problem with the naturalist philosophy is that it does not correspond to "freethinking" unless *free* refers an untethering from

---

8. Jones, *Why Does God Allow Evil?*, 12.

9. The philosophical belief that everything arises from natural properties and causes, and supernatural or spiritual explanations are excluded or discounted.

10. Harris, "Free Will."

truth or reality. If our reality is purely a psychological construction by chemical function, we would not be able to trust its assessment of higher-level concepts such as truth, justice, or even our perception of reality itself. Theologian Alvin Plantinga explains that naturalism is a concept that conflicts with principles of science, suggesting that if naturalism is true "our cognitive faculties have been cobbled together by natural selection."[11]

Therefore, those who embrace naturalism cannot offer evidence of a Darwinian process offering reliable human cognition beyond an instinct of self-preservation. Plantinga argues that the probability of our faculties being reliable is low if naturalism and evolution were true. This same proposition applies to the implied legitimacy of naturalism and evolution as well, both being man-made concepts.

Plantinga writes,

> So, my belief that naturalism and evolution are true gives me a defeater for that very belief; that belief shoots itself in the foot and is self-referentially incoherent; therefore, I cannot rationally accept it. And if one can't accept both naturalism and evolution, that pillar of current science, then there is serious conflict between naturalism and science.[12]

Are we robots and slaves to DNA, or do humans have free will? The evidence aligns more with theism than naturalism. Biblical scripture states that man is made in God's image (Genesis 1: 26–27) and whose purpose includes worshiping God with all aspect of our being, including our mind, our soul, and our spirit (Mark 12:30). If naturalism is true, chemical reactions guide us for the purpose of self-preservation, not on truth, justice, or morality. As Richard Dawkins explains, "DNA neither knows nor cares. DNA just is. And we dance to its music."[13]

Furthermore, even some atheists recognize the psychological danger of pushing unsubstantiated propaganda regarding the

---

11. Plantinga, *Where the Conflict Really Lies*, 314.
12. Plantinga, *Where the Conflict Really Lies*, 314.
13. Dawkins, *A River out of Eden*, 133.

The Diagnosis—A Theological Inoculation

concept of free will. Philosopher Daniel Dennett explains that popularizing this unscientifically verified claim is ill-considered and potentially doing real harm in modern society today.[14] He uses the example of a fictional neuroscientist who implants a chip to counteract the effects of Obsessive Compulsive Disorder in a patient (a legitimate medical procedure in use today) but the physician tells the patient that in stabilizing the OCD, he also has the ability to control the patient's will; the patient no longer has intellectual control over his decisions.

As a result of the patient accepting this information, his normal emotional state changes to self-indulgent, aggressive, and even criminal. Dennett explains this scenario, while purely fictional, is clearly professionally unethical and irresponsible. He argues, the same applies to popularizing this unproven concept in cyberspace today regarding the absence of free will. He references the work of author and researcher Kathleen D. Vohs and psychologist Jonathan W. Schooler that demonstrate the negative impact that acceptance of determinism (the claim that the human mind does not have free will) has on the human mind.[15] The experiments showed a reduction of ethical decisions by people who embraced this premise.

The atheist worldview seems to be a bundle of contradictions. One cannot bring that philosophy into harmony with itself and given that level of internal conflict, the worldview fails. The indefensible claims of the worldview of the non-theist are also not just benign; they can be harmful and irresponsible.

The science and medical community clearly understand the psychological implications of medicine as suggested by the placebo effect.[16] Belief has warrant. However, even from a purely secular and utilitarian perspective, given the multitude of evidence which shows the positive impact of religious belief on humans,[17] the majority of those who embrace scientism, humanism, and atheism

---

14. Dennett, "The Nefarious Neurosurgeon."
15. Vohs and Schooler, "The Value of Believing," 49–54.
16. Defined as the phenomenon that some people experience a benefit after a medically inactive, yet patient-perceived, curative treatment.
17. Phillips, "A Re-examination," 299–311.

still aggressively attack religious ideology. This perspective is difficult to rationalize as being truly objective, nor is it appropriately influenced by the scientific method. It seems some may not want to truly follow the evidence where it leads, when the evidence conflicts with biased personal ideology.

INADEQUATE APOLOGETIC FOUNDATION

While the research participants were equally distributed into two groups from a self-assessment of the depth of their Christian beliefs prior to deconversion, it was clear that both groups (those who claimed their Christianity was deeply rooted vs those who claimed a moderate embrace of Christian doctrine) were equally vulnerable to apostasy. As they experienced their intellectual or emotional challenges, their Christian faith could not withstand the assault. This section evaluates the apparent inadequacy of the apologetic foundation for modern Christians.

To address the ideologically vulnerable, it appears the church and the Christian apologist must prioritize reinforcing the fundamental religious presuppositions regarding the transcendent. To the apostate, once the presupposition about the existence of God is removed, the remaining historical, theological, and philosophical evidence of Christianity becomes highly questionable at best, and completely indefensible at worst.

Throughout history and across all religious spectrums, religions tend to be defined by practices and not just beliefs. Therein lies the fundamental flaw in the perspective of modern Christians regarding presuppositional apologetics. The spiritual algorithm of the liberal Christian is flawed. To the average liberal Christian, faith equals devotion to ritual and therefore by extension, makes one feel that they are working hard enough to earn redemption. This formula does not have biblical support, nor does it have a Christ-centered basis (Ephesians 2:8–9).

Jesus constantly engaged with the Jewish religious elite, challenging their shortsighted and hypocritical display of religiosity. Psychologist and theologian J. Harold Ellens explains that Jesus

The Diagnosis—A Theological Inoculation

was intolerant of this adulteration of God's covenant with humanity. He writes, "[Jesus] constantly attacked the Pharisees and their proposals for renewing the spiritual vitality of the Jewish Community. He constantly and intentionally provoked conflict and disruption of the status quo, spiritually and politically. He refused to negotiate, compromise, palliate, or mollify his insistence upon keeping his elbow perpetually in the eye of the people in power."[18]

Ellens further explains Jesus's intention in assertively confronting the religious leaders of the day. "His principle was simply that the renewal of Jewish spirituality could only come from a return to the Abrahamic Covenant," which declared God's love for humanity unconditional from our behavior which then allows man to be removed from the burden of fear, guilt, and shame from the equation of our relationship with the Creator (Genesis 12; Romans 8, Micah 7:18–20). "He saw that the Pharisees and Scribes were absolutely wrong in assuming that the Mosaic legal system would renew the Jewish relationship with God."[19]

The modern church congregant seems to have fallen into this same trap. This is a trap that presupposes that one can somehow determine, define, and obtain their own redemption. This formula for secular redemption places a heavy burden on humanity as the dependent variable. Humanity neither has this capacity nor can bear this burden. Most deconverts in this research described the constant "pressure" that they felt as Christians. To them, the church was pressuring them to obtain an unobtainable goal.

Christianity offers a spiritual algorithm that is unique in that it addresses humanity's moral gap and search for truth, meaning, and purpose, the yearning in our soul. The presuppositional "God Math" algorithm is stated as follows:

$$U + (\square - God) > 1.[20]$$

Stated non-numerically, you, plus anything other than God, is less than whole, and therefore, incomplete. On a social level, one is unable to have a basis for their own morality. On a psychological

---

18. Ellens, "That Tough Guy," 1–6.
19. Ellens, "That Tough Guy," 6–8.
20. "God Math" algorithm formulated by J. Childress in 2020.

level, one will always struggle to find fulfillment and balance in isolation. On a theological level, one cannot achieve redemption on their own; however, Scripture promises that through Christ, humanity is capable of doing anything, including achieving personal fulfillment, victory, and meaning (Philippians 4:13).

The Judeo-Christian worldview, the entirety of the biblical scripture, and the entirety of Christ's message is based on this main premise. If one does not embrace this core belief, a person's ideological algorithm is wrong, their beliefs are based on shifting sand, and what remains is simply a self-constructed worldview with flawed input and flawed output. Even if decorated with the rituals of quasi-Christianity, the self-constructed worldview is vulnerable to collapse from any strong wind of culture and society. Any attempt to replace God with any other variable (i.e., good deeds, giving money to the church, acquiescence to culture) and the math fails.

A person is not able to obtain their own redemption—not as a churchgoer, not as a religious believer, not as a "good" Christian, not as a Jewish Pharisee, and certainly not as a secular member of a cancel-culture, name-calling, label-applying, race-baiting, Marxism-espousing, tribal, no-hope, no-meaning, subjective morality, postmodern culture. One soon finds that the self-righteous Christian attempts to consume a non-sustaining diet. Ironically, in regard to today's post-modern culture, they eat their own.[21]

Regarding the critical apologetic aspects of the Judeo-Christian God presupposition, many define *presupposition* as "assumed without proof." Regardless of the semantical attacks and claims of wishful thinking, the Christian church has rock-solid ground to continue to treat this core belief as unquestionable and axiomatic. However, for the deconvert participants in our research, the God presupposition was the single pivot point from belief to unbelief.

The great learning for the church is as follows: the fundamental presuppositions can and should be considered axiomatic; however, these presuppositions must also be actively taught, explained, apologetically defended, and reinforced amongst the church body.

---

21. Pitts, "A Liberal Marxism?," 235–42.

The Diagnosis—A Theological Inoculation

Just because something is unquestionable and ineffable does not mean it is inexplicable or indefensible. Therefore, the church itself is the first mission field for the ministry of Christian apologetics.

Some suggest the gap between science and religion is fact versus faith. Yet, the scientist has his own presuppositions. Rabbi and author Harold S. Kushner, in paralleling the faith that believers have in God with the faith that scientists have in postmodernity, explains:

> Because when they look into their microscopes, they see things happening which can only happen if quarks and electrons existed (meaning if they were observable). I believe in the reality of God in the way that scientists believe in the reality of electrons. I see things that would not happen unless there is a God.[22]

History may prove that one of the greatest proponents of presuppositional apologetics is author and scholar, Greg Bahnsen. While some would not align with the Calvinist perspective of Bahnsen, his interpretation of presuppositionalist apologetics, originated with Dutch American Christian Philosopher Cornelius Van Til, is notable.

Bahnsen died tragically of heart disease at age forty-seven, but authored many books on this topic, including the posthumously credited work, *Presuppositional Apologetics*. Amongst the edited notes, discovered fifteen years after the passing of Bahnsen, included the following declarative for the presuppositional apologist:

> The very question of whether God might exist, or Scripture might be true, is tantamount to a denial about what Scripture says about God's inescapably clear and authoritative revelation. To attempt an apologetic which takes an (allegedly) impartial starting point and method is to radically deny the existence of the Christian God as described in His nature and activities by Scripture.

---

22. Kushner, *Nine Essential*, 22.

In this exhortation, Bahnsen was not discrediting the purpose of apologetics, but rather he was challenging the mindset of the apologist himself. In Bahnsen's perspective, it is impossible to remove God from the algorithm and then argue our way toward God from a perspective of possibility, probability, or preponderance of the evidence. Man is completely incapable of evaluating the reality of God using our finite and flawed cognitive processes. God is beyond the natural and His being is beyond our ability to comprehend or explain.

Bahnsen ultimately rejects that the unbeliever's argument against God is evidential. There is separate motivation for the unbeliever which must be understood and unashamedly addressed. He writes,

> We do not present Christianity as a "hypothesis" to be verified, and we are repulsed by the idea of presenting men with a "probability" to worship. Our apologetic must presuppose Christ's Word in Scripture, casting down all reasoning that exalts itself against God. We must use the tools supplied by the Holy Spirit, not the devices of sin. We must seriously recognize that the sinner's problem in rejecting the Bible is ethical, not intellectual. Only regeneration can bring a man to believe, and apologetic argument must never presume to preempt or in any way take the place of regeneration.[23]

Bahnsen's encouragement to the apologist to maintain the proper mindset is credible. Certainly, his instruction to recognize the appropriate role of the apologist in relation to the role of the Holy Spirit is undeniable. However, it must be noted that intellectual rejection of the existence of God is the central aspect of the deconversion process.

The reason behind the rejection seems indeed to be morally grounded but the end result is simply an intellectual rejection of God. The apologist can have an influential role at this point, but he must approach this situation with proper intellectual and spiritual

---

23. Bahnsen, *Presuppositional Apologetics*, 14.

preparation—along with a proper understanding of the spiritual and psychological status of their interlocutor.

There are two great questions to which one must contend as they wrestle with the transcendent: 1) How does a non-theist ground their claim of morality in the absence of a Creator-God as the only viable source of objective morality? 2) What evidence do they have for an alternative that is stronger than the evidence of the life, death, and resurrection of Jesus Christ?

Regarding the historical evidence for the resurrection of Jesus, New Testament scholar (and now a self-described agnostic who was previously an Evangelical Christian) Bart Ehrman states:

> That Jesus' followers (and later Paul) had resurrection experiences is, in my judgment, a fact. What the reality was that gave rise to the experiences I do not know. Paul's tradition that 500 people saw Jesus at the same time has led some people to suggest that Jesus' followers suffered mass hysteria. But mass hysteria does not explain the other traditions. Finally, we know that after his death his followers experienced what they described as the 'resurrection': the appearance of a living but transformed person who had actually died. They believed this, they lived it, and they died for it.[24]

German New Testament scholar Gerd Lüdemann agrees with this perspective as well:

> After Jesus' death, the disciples endured persecution, and a number of them experienced martyrdom. The strength of their conviction indicates that they were not just claiming Jesus had appeared to them after rising from the dead. They really believed it. They willingly endangered themselves by publicly proclaiming the risen Christ.[25]

Theologian and author N.T. Wright also mirrors these opinions:

---

24. Ehrman, *Jesus: Apocalyptic Prophet*, 230–31.
25. Ludemann, *What Really Happened?*, 80.

> We are left with the conclusion that the combination of empty tomb and appearances of the living Jesus forms a set of circumstances which is itself *both necessary and sufficient* for the rise of early Christian belief. Without these phenomena, we cannot explain why this belief came into existence, and took the shape it did. With them, we can explain it exactly and precisely.[26]

The death, burial, and resurrection of Jesus Christ is the basis of Christian belief and without those historical events occurring, Christianity fails (I Corinthians 15:14). The historical evidence is substantively and broadly supported by the worldwide community of New Testament scholars. The atheist not only fails to offer credible evidence against the historicity of the events, but they also fail to explain the historic growth of Christianity *without* those events occurring.

If indeed the atheist is as open minded as they suggest, if they truly have intention to follow the evidence where it leads, then they must recognize that their worldview carries the greater risk from an eschatological perspective. If the Christian worldview is wrong, people have lost nothing more than an attempt to bring attention to the source of objective moral values and duties to society in establishing a bridge to the transcendent. If the atheist is wrong, they are wrong about society, morality, the human condition, the reality of meaning, the source of truth, the existence of the supernatural realm, and the eternal implications for their own soul.

Ultimately, the greatest loss for the atheist is the opportunity to establish a personal relationship with someone who still powerfully influences our world 2000 years later. An honest assessment by the atheist should be to take more seriously the evidence of the Christian worldview until such time that positive evidence is established for atheism. Until that time occurs, they have no evidence to rule out the transcendent implications of a worldview that has proven benefits on a societal level as well as proven benefits on a personal psychological level.

---

26. Wright, "The New Unimproved Jesus."

The Diagnosis—A Theological Inoculation

Without exception, among the interviewed apostates, there was no new evidence against the resurrection of Jesus; there was no new evidence against the existence of God; there was no new evidence to suggest the unreliability of the Bible (although the interviewees offered ample evidence to suggest the Bible was inconsistent with the "morals" of modern culture and society). There were claims of biblical and theistic immorality, but the anecdotal examples provided were strawman claims and blatant misinterpretations of primarily Old Testament warfare situations and Mosaic Law.

Machen describes why the authority of Bible must be a critical element of the Christian base of presuppositions. He completely discounts the claim that dependence on a book is a dead or artificial thesis. He gives evidence of how the Great Reformation of the sixteenth century was based on the defense of biblical truth and it changed the course of human thinking toward philosophy, religion, and morality. He compares the basis of a foundation on the transcendent versus the foundation of human creation:

> Dependence upon a word of man would be slavish, but dependence upon God's word is life. Dark and gloomy would be the world, if it were left to our own devices, and had no blessed word of God. The Bible, to the Christian, is not a burdensome law, but the very Magna Carta of Christian liberty. It is no wonder then, that liberalism is totally different from Christianity, for the foundation is different. Christianity is founded upon the Bible. It bases upon the Bible both its thinking and its life. Liberalism, on the other hand is founded upon the shifting emotions of sinful men.[27]

It should be concerning that, without any supporting evidence, a professing Christian could turn their back so easily on their religious faith. Certainly, there is biblical evidence to suggest that some people claim the label of "Christian" without truly understanding what it means to experience Christ with a total commitment of their lives to Him (Matthew 7:21–23). They commit

---

27. Machen, *Christianity and Liberalism*, 78–9.

their money, they commit their time, they commit emotionally (which can be dangerously deceiving and superficial in itself), and sometimes they commit intellectually; but few understand the true depth of the commitment as explained by Jesus—the result is a superficial commitment at best, which is intellectually feeble and spiritually vulnerable.

Loving God with all your heart (intensely), with your soul (sincerely), and with all your strength (energetically and with all of one's faculties) results in the death of self. When self is crucified, Christ is glorified. This is yet another amazing dichotomy of Christianity. In dying to self, and in sacrifice to Christ, one can achieve personal fulfillment, meaning, and clarity of purpose. "Therefore, if anyone is in Christ, he is a new creation. The old things have passed away. Behold, all things have become new" (1 Corinthians 5:17).

One must understand that this is a constant battle, a truly spiritual battle. In giving one's heart, soul, and mind to Christ, note that the mind is not spiritually sealed from attack, as is the soul. The soul is under spiritual safe keeping (John 10:27–29; Romans 8:38–39; John 3:16; Colossians 3:3). However, there is a warning about the fragility and vulnerability of the mind. As Paul admonishes, "Therefore, I urge you brothers and sisters, by the mercies of God, to present your bodies as a living and holy sacrifice, acceptable to God, which is your spiritual service of worship. And do not be conformed to this world, but be transformed by the renewing of your mind, so that you may prove what the will of God is, that which is good and acceptable and perfect" (Romans 12:1–2).

Research, study, devotion, and meditation on biblical scripture is a critical aspect of this journey of spiritual maturity. Renewal is a process, not a project. The tense of the verb suggests an ongoing journey, not an end state. The mind is the most vulnerable aspect of the Triune being of humanity. As a result, the Christian can be vulnerable to the shifting sands and blowing winds of culture. The enemy knows this and the political left senses it.

The embrace of postmodern thought, of moral relativism, of so-called social justice, of socialism, and of religious pluralism is

The Diagnosis—A Theological Inoculation

prevalent within the Christian church today. Belief in a transcendent Creator-God is one of the few core beliefs that separates the two ideologies of the political left and the Christian left.

Religious "Nones" are the largest religious group among Democrats and Democrat-leaning Pew survey respondents (See Figure 1). Younger generations attend church less, read the Bible less, and pray less than older generations (See Figure 2). Democrat and left-leaning Christians read the Bible less, have more doubt about God's existence, attend church less, and pray less than Republican and conservative-leaning Christians[28] (See Figure 3).

Religious 'Nones' Now Largest Single Religious Group Among Democrats

Religious identity of self-identified Democrats and Democratic-leaning adults

	Evangelical Prot.	Mainline Prot.	Historically black Prot.	Catholic	Other Christian groups	Non-Christian faiths	Unaffiliated
2014	16%	13	12	21	2 8		28
2007	19	17	11	24	2 7		19

Christian: 63% (2014)
Christian: 74% (2007)

Source: 2014 Religious Landscape Study, conducted June 4-Sept. 30, 2014. Those who said "don't know" or did not give an answer are not shown.

PEW RESEARCH CENTER

One could easily challenge the theological basis of someone who claims the label of Christian but questions the authority of the Bible, while entertaining the shifting tenets of modern culture. These are disparate and unreconcilable platforms. The atheist, while claiming a pursuit of rationality, seems curiously led by social predisposition instead of truth. One of the most notable atheists of the past fifty years and historically prolific anti-theist, Antony Flew, famously renounced his atheism by quoting Socrates, explaining that he was simply "following the evidence where it led."[29] The last years of his life were dedicated to a pursuit of theism.

---

28. Pew Report, "*US Public Becoming Less Religious.*"
29. Flew, *There is a God*, 89.

People in Older Generational Cohorts Increasingly Rely on Religion for Guidance on Questions of Right and Wrong

	Rely most on religious teachings/beliefs on questions of right/wrong	Read scripture at least once a week	Participate in prayer/scripture study group at least once a week	Say "my religion is one true faith leading to eternal life"
	%	%	%	%
Silent generation (born 1928-1945)				
2007	34	42	28	20
2014	41	44	32	23
Change	+7	+2	+4	+3
Baby Boomers (born 1946-1964)				
2007	31	36	23	18
2014	38	38	27	21
Change	+7	+2	+4	+3
Generation X (born 1965-1980)				
2007	28	31	21	20
2014	33	36	25	20
Change	+5	+5	+4	0
Older Millennials (born 1981-1989)				
2007	24	27	20	22
2014	26	29	18	19
Change	+2	+2	-2	-3
Younger Millennials (born 1990-1996)				
2007	n/a	n/a	n/a	n/a
2014	23	25	18	22
Change	n/a	n/a	n/a	n/a

Source: 2014 Religious Landscape Study, conducted June 4–Sept. 30, 2014.
PEW RESEARCH CENTER

As for the Christian apologist, he should stand firm. The believer has no reason to be ashamed of truth (Galatians 5:1; Deuteronomy 32: 31; Psalm 18:1–3; 2 Samuel 2:22). Truth passes all tests and vetting—propaganda fails every test of credibility and legitimacy. However, the professing Christian must inventory his true beliefs. God's existence and Christ's resurrection is the greatest possible news for this world. We may be the miracle that our atheist neighbor needs. We cannot save them, but we have been instructed to *tell* them. A Christian surely would spring to action if a person's life were in danger; yet, we flinch, or even completely retreat, given the fact that their soul is at risk.

One could claim the atheist is a lost cause due to the depth of their anger, resentment, and rejection of the Gospel; however, the evidence suggests otherwise. C.S. Lewis was once an avowed atheist and became arguably the greatest Christian apologist of the twentieth century. Philosopher, and at one point, the most famous atheist on the planet, Antony Flew renounced his atheism late in

The Diagnosis—A Theological Inoculation

life and penned the book, *There is a God*. Christian apologist Josh McDowell was a former atheist, as was geneticist and Director of the National Genome project, Francis Collins; as was Harvard Law School Founder, Simon Greenleaf; as was best-selling Christian author, Lee Strobel. Even more importantly, while the depth of anti-theistic passion may not have been the same as atheists avow today, at one point, so was every Christian.

Even the atheist, all while flailing in emotional denial, ultimately respects the steadfast Christian standing firm on presuppositional ground. Author, columnist, and cultural commentator Larry Taunton discussed this surprising perspective as he wrote about his 2010 debate with one of the most famous members of the so-called New Atheists, Christopher Hitchens. While Hitchens was a renowned source of vulgar and repulsive comments about Christians and Christianity, he noted how Taunton was spared the usual vile rhetoric, so he asked Hichens about his abnormal degree of respect and reserve. Hichens reply was "because you believe it."

Taunton gave another example of a peer at Dartmouth who said, "I really can't consider a Christian a good, moral person if he isn't trying to convert me."[30] Taunton continues:

> As surprising as it may seem, this sentiment is not as unusual as you might think. It finds resonance in the well-publicized comments of Penn Jillette, the atheist illusionist and comedian: "I don't respect people who don't proselytize. I don't respect that at all. If you believe that there's a heaven and hell and people could be going to hell or not getting eternal life or whatever, and you think that it's not really worth telling them this because it would make it socially awkward . . . How much do you have to hate somebody to believe that everlasting life is possible and not tell them that?"[31]

In addition to not being reluctant to the process of apologetics, the Christian apologist should also not be shy as to the foundational arguments, such as feeling restricted to defending the

---

30. Taunton, "Listening to Young Atheists."
31. Taunton, "Listening to Young Atheists."

Theistic presupposition purely on supernatural grounds. Antony Flew explains the rationale behind his quite famous conversion from atheism to Theism:

> I must stress that my discovery of the Divine has proceeded purely on a natural level, without any reference to supernatural phenomena. It has been an exercise in what is traditionally called natural theology. It has had no connection with any of the revealed religions. Nor do I claim to have any personal experience of God or any experience that may be called supernatural or miraculous. In short, my discovery of the Divine has been a pilgrimage of reason and not of faith.[32]

In essence, one can obtain evidence of the transcendent simply with evidence of transcendent's impact on the observable world. As is the case with the theoretical quark, known only by its effects and influence on its surroundings, the impact of the observable by that which is unobservable, is difficult to rationally deny.

ADDRESSING OBJECTIONS TO CHRISTIANITY

It may be difficult to change someone's mind after such an extreme worldview shift as deconversion. As a result, the church must become more aware of the intellectual objections to Christianity and equip discipleship training and apologetics programs to address how these deconversion decisions are made. Most of the deconversion process took a long time to manifest into a final rejection of faith. This reflects a missed opportunity by church leadership and lay personnel in recognizing congregants who were actively in a spiritual struggle while they were still attending church.

Negative experiences with other Christians were commonly referenced by those who deconverted. Authenticity is deemed lacking amongst modern Christians, while judgmentalism and hypocrisy is rampant. Certainly, some of the accusations against Christians are due to nonbelievers rejecting the message of Christ

---

32. Flew, *There is a God*, 93.

and by doing so, they fallaciously strawman the church, the Bible, Christianity, and Christians themselves. In defense of the attempts to attack religion, there is ample anecdotal evidence of legitimate moral failures of followers of Christ. There is no promise that Christianity will force someone to become a better person.

The fact that even the believer is flawed and prone to failure is proof that humanity needs a Savior. Regardless of the ideological camp in which one may reside, humans are flawed vessels, in constant need of repair and redemption. Regardless, Christ did not come to make bad people good. He came to make dead people live.[33]

The ethical and moral failures of the Christian is not evidence in support of atheism, nor against Christianity, no more than the failure of a student is the fault of the school. Yet, this perspective should be a wakeup call to the Christian. The ultimate Christian apologetic is the life of the believer and its reflection of Christ.[34] If belief in Christ is not true-enough, transformative-enough, and valuable-enough to make a noticeable change in the believer's life, why should the non-believer bother? If this describes the life of a person claiming commitment to Christ, a re-evaluation of their true commitment is warranted. One cannot earn their way to redemption; a life exemplifying Christ is evidence of—not the basis of—its legitimate commitment and transformation (Romans 3:27–28).

The church, or any other earthly entity, was not designed as a proxy for a relationship with Jesus (John 14:6). The purpose and role of the church must be correctly understood for someone to have proper expectations and therefore become resilient to church-related failures and disappointments.

Defined clearly among the pillars of Existentialism[35] and reinforced from a naturalist and Darwinian evolution perspective,

---

33. Tarrants, "True Conversions and Wholehearted Commitment."

34. Craig, *Reasonable Faith*, 407.

35. Existentialism is defined as a philosophical theory or approach which emphasizes the existence of the individual person as a free and responsible agent determining their own development through acts of the will.

the concepts of hope, meaning, and justice are simply human constructs.[36] Existentialists believe that reality exists only in one's mind (the concept of *isolation*). The philosophy also suggests there is no meaning in life. Death is the inevitable conclusion for all humans. People can have impact on the course of their lives; however, it is minuscule.

On existentialism and similar worldviews, people are simply organic slaves to their DNA. As a result, abstract and intangible qualities such as meaning, purpose, value, and ethics have no basis in a world driven only by the random whims of natural selection. These claims are the antithesis of biblical scripture (Romans 15:4; Proverbs 24:14; Job 11:18; Jeremiah 29:11; 2 Corinthians 3:12–14).

Atheist philosopher Kai Nielsen challenges the inability for secular humanity to rationalize and justify the existence of objective morality. He assaults the concept of immoralism[37] and he confronts the flawed presupposition that one is truly able to understand what it means to claim that something is right or wrong, nor that we have the means to determine what is right or wrong.

> The picture I have painted for you is not a pleasant one. Reflection on it depresses me. I detest, as much as any of you, such lack of moral integrity as one finds in immoralism. Indeed, reflecting on this picture and taking it to heart fortifies my own resolve to engage in social struggle, to do my utmost to do my bit to bring about a world in which genuine moral community will become possible and the class of immoralists, including of course classic amoralists, will wither away or at least dwindle with the social circumstances not being so conductive to their flourishing.[38]

Finally, and most challenging to the non-theist, Nielsen challenges the claim that humanity can reason its way to morality. In

---

36. Lazarus, "The Depressing Truth?"

37. A system of thought which rejects the existence of morality principles, certainly of conventional and traditional pillars of morality. Variations of this belief system were posited by Friedrich Nietzsche. See Benn, "The Morals of an Immoralist-Friedrich Nietzsche," 1–23.

38. Nielsen, "Why Should I Be Moral?," 90–91.

The Diagnosis—A Theological Inoculation

his opinion, the human species lacks the ability to establish unbiased and resolute caring for all human life (he uses the term, "disinterested," relating an appropriate analogy like the image of the blindfolded *Lady Justice* of American jurisprudence, dispassionately and without prejudice, applying the law to society):

> There is a great philosophical lesson here which perhaps also has human import. The point is, pure, practical reason, even with a good knowledge of the facts, will not take you to morality. You cannot reason or even bargain with yourself with a moral commitment such that you will come clearly and correctly to acknowledge that there must have been a failing of reason on your part if you are not a person of good will, a person of moral integrity. Underlying morality, for it to be what it purports to be, there must be a persuasive attitude of disinterested caring for all human life (and perhaps for all sentient creatures)—the smallest as well as the greatest of us.[39]

The implications are clear—these ideals are only possible across the entirety of the human species, given the transcendent. Meaning, purpose, truth, morality, and justice have a universal basis only if God exists and only through Him (Matthew 6:25–33).

Furthermore, the atheist has a clear hierarchy of values, so even with an attempt to balance a definition of morality across disparate cultural, religious, and philosophical pillars, they will ultimately default to secular version of monotheism, which returns to a key premise of this book—the self. The prioritization of self will eventually overrule other values, which by default, relinquishes macro culture and macro values to the status of lesser gods, subservient to the micro god of self and Darwinist self-preservation.

The premise of secular objective morality shows no evidence of successfully establishing, nor influencing, universal moral principles. Secular morality does seek personal moral redemption. Modern society devotes so much time and money on the pollution in our environment but we so little time on the pollution in our minds. A science book that is twenty years old is virtually outdated

---

39. Nielsen, *Why Should I Be Moral?*, 91.

in the twenty-first century, but the philosophical and theological writings of Aristotle, Plato, and Descartes, not to mention Augustine, Irenaeus, and Aquinas, are still as applicable today as they were in the second and third centuries. Modern society devalues morality as a fundamental tenet of a progressive worldview and therefore posits morality as an insufficient arbiter for secular culture.

Admittedly, the existentialist does attempt to establish a humanistic basis for this premise. Psychologist Ralph Lewis, author of *Finding Purpose in a Godless World* explains in a recent article for *Psychology Today*:

> The universe may not be purposeful, but humans are. Our sense of purpose is not at all dependent on the universe having a purpose. All living creatures are purposive, in a basic sense. Even a bacterium or a plant is purpose-driven. Human purposive behavior has evolved to become much more embellished, elaborated by conscious intention, but it is fundamentally driven by the same basic instinctual goals of all living things: survival and reproduction.[40]

The existentialists fail to explain *how* one can derive morality, meaning, and purpose from a Darwinian perspective of species driven by survival and flourishing. For example, there is no contribution to human flourishing by the act of abortion. "Women's rights" is the claim to justify the action, even to the ultimate demise of the fetus, but one could make the same tone-deaf claim about rape. It accomplishes the purpose of propagation of the species with an even greater benefit of no loss of life in the process. The argument need not apply only a female perspective. Certainly, no one would defend the rape premise in defense of male Darwinian-driven choice, and neither should the premise apply to abortion. As a result, the existentialist logic fails normal reason.

Moreover, Lewis's comments are an example of the tendency for the atheist, naturalist, and existentialist to borrow from the Christian worldview. Concepts such as "good" and "evil" do not

40. Lewis, "Purpose, Meaning and Morality."

The Diagnosis—A Theological Inoculation

exist in a Darwinian world. What remains is simply one person's perspective of morality, meaning, and purpose which has no universal authority or prospect for universal adoption.

There will be some aspects of theistic and biblical truth that differ from one's personal preferences. It should be expected. Human disagreement with Christ-centered, biblical principles do not stand as evidence against the existence of God; it stands only evidence of one's dislike of God. However, if God is God, is it that surprising that the omniscient Creator has knowledge, judgment, and perspective that the creation does not have?

This thesis suggests it would be more surprising that the creation had complete intellectual synthesis with the Creator, just as it would be surprising if the child had a complete intellectual synthesis with the parent. The environment, cultural, and intellectual capacity delta between the two are immeasurable. "For my thoughts are not your thoughts and my ways are not your ways" (Isaiah 55:8).

So, when someone (without the expected tendency to strawman the Bible) evaluates truth in Scripture and it goes against their politics, or their cultural influence, or their assessment of "morality," the creation should take note and reevaluate the reason for the discrepancy. It seems indefensible that a Darwinist-driven intellect would have the morality integrity or the intellectual capacity to cast judgement on the Creator.

Another common claim against the existence of the transcendent, certainly against the possible existence of a "loving" God, is the existence of evil. Disappointments, failures, heartaches, and struggles exist in life. There are no biblical promises to the contrary. If one claims the existence of evil is evidence against God, solace will certainly not be found in a Darwinist-centered, naturalist worldview. There is no solution to the problem of evil in atheism. Furthermore, the atheist, if he stays true to evolutionary theory, has no basis to define good versus evil, objective morality, or moral duties.[41]

---

41. Craig, *Reasonable Faith*, 175.

With the gift of free-will comes the prospect of the choice of evil. Various noted apologists explain that there could only have been one of four worlds that God could have created. First, God could have chosen to not create any world. Second, God could have chosen to create a world where there was no evil, a form of robotic intellectual restriction of the mind. Third, God could have created a world where people would only choose good over evil; a second version of robotic control of the mind. The final option is that God could have created this world; a world where humanity has the greatest gift of all, the gift of free, unfettered choice between good and evil. For such apologists, only in this world, in a world where we have the free will to accept or reject God, is it possible for the greatest ethic to exist—love.[42]

God gave us the opportunity to experience the greatest possible ethic, but this gift also carries a great risk. Evil is a privation of good, just as darkness is a privation of light. It has no source of existence on its own. Evil does not have a proper ontological basis.[43]

Regardless of arguments regarding the origination of evil, any claim of God being the author of evil must provide evidence against the possibility that God would not have a valid reason for allowing the privation of good through free will. It is certainly possible that the design of this world is optimized to draw the largest possible percentage of humanity to Him, the objective standard of good, while still preserving the gift of free will.[44]

The atheist fails to realize that God's plan, allowing the possibility of evil because of free will, is the very vehicle itself which allows them to question God in the first place.

---

42. See philosopher Gottfried Leibniz and biblical scholar Alvin Plantinga, et al.

43. Jones, *Why Does God Allow Evil?*, 19–22.

44. Craig, *On-Guard*, 155.

5

Learning for the Church— The Toughest Apologetic

CERTAINLY, THE HIGH VOLUME of Christian deconversion reflects the severity of spiritual warfare occurring today, but it also reflects a huge gap in the modern Christian church's strategy and approach to discipleship. The modern church has twenty-first century audio-visuals, twenty-first century marketing and advertising, and twenty-first century appeal to the "seeker." While the modern mega-church has mastered the ability to draw a big crowd, they fall desperately short in building disciples who can intellectually combat cultural and societal attacks on core Christian doctrine.[1] This section will address key learnings from the deconversion research for the modern church.

Many deconverted Christians become actively affiliated with atheist organizations. While deconversion certainly reflects a rejection of fundamental Judeo-Christian principles, many former Christians seem to retain the desire for community, interpersonal fellowship, and group validation of ideological identity that they enjoyed as self-professed Christians. The individual benefit from communal interaction and support is generally considered one

---

1. Marriott, *A Recipe for Disaster*, 12.

of the primary utilitarian functions of the Christian church, but negative church experiences are also often blamed as a reason for their rejection of Christianity.

The process of establishing a proper apologetic to a deconverted Christian must begin with an understanding of the personal experience which drove them away from the church and their faith. It is doubtful that attempts at intellectual, philosophical, or theological introspection will be effective without this grounding. If someone has been spiritually and ideologically derailed because of one event or situation, it would seem possible to overcome with an equally powerful positive experience.

A church that has a strong program of relationship and discipleship (small-group home meetings, personal follow-up and prayer time, on-going Christian education, and so on) can effectively rebuild that bridge. Reaction to an anecdotal event does not have to result in a total rejection of Christ. However, the challenge is much easier to recognize these vulnerable congregants prior to their final embrace of outright apostasy.

The twenty-first century Christian church has many challenges, both internal and external. The church must stand firm on biblical principles while still demonstrating Christ's love for humanity. It is critical for the church in confronting modern culture to find a proper balance between relevance and influence. The church must be relevant in a postmodern society where Christianity is demonized, while also working to differentiate Christianity in a positive way from the cultural norms. Many churches attempt to commercialize the Christian message for greater societal reception.

Nineteenth century theologian B.F. Westcott explains the impact of such spiritual propaganda: "We have so persistently dissembled the power of the Gospel . . . that it is pardonable if those who judge of it by us should doubt whether it is anything more efficacious and inspiring than the pathetic guesses which adore the writings of philosophy."[2]

---

2. Westcott, *Gospel of the Resurrection*, 24.

The challenge is how to increase the church's societal footprint while simultaneously honoring the truth of the Gospel of Jesus Christ. The church has one commission from Jesus — go and preach the gospel. The Great Commission contains no clause that prompts consideration of a version of the Gospel that may be more palatable, more acceptable, or more politically correct. Jesus Christ exhorted His followers to preach the true, unadulterated Gospel to the world (Matthew 28:16-20).

THE DECONVERTED SEEK A REPLACEMENT RELIGION

"The problem of disbelieving in God is not that a man ends up believing nothing. Alas, it is much worse. He ends up believing anything."[3] It is obvious from the research that apostates now seek alternative gods to worship in place of their former Deity. Everyone has a basis of value and a moral system. The apostates claim the removal of God from the top of their hierarchy of values; still, they seek a replacement source. Research from the interviews suggest clear doctrinal principles for the deconverted Christian and their new religion.

Atheist author and poet Charles Bukowski stated, "For those who believe in God, most of the big questions are answered. But for those of us who can't readily accept the God formula, the big answers don't remain stone-written. We adjust to new conditions and discoveries. We are pliable. Love need not be a command nor faith a dictum. I am my own god."[4]

As previously stated, if one does not believe that God exists, then a search begins for a replacement deity. The self, whether defined by an explicit conviction to follow personal desires, or whether it is a replacement wrapped in a cloak of legitimacy (such as political activism) is elevated in a futile attempt by the nonbeliever to fulfill the inherent desire to seek purpose and meaning.

---

3. Cammaerts, *The Laughing Prophet*, 37.
4. Haught, *2000 Years of Disbelief*, 293.

The self is the most convenient deity; unfortunately, it is also the most hollow, empty, futile, and ineffectual god that someone could conjure.

Whether guided by Darwinian instincts of self-preservation and survival or whether driven by the desire for post-modern denial of the transcendent, if one eliminates the prospect of objective meaning and moral truth, what remains is simply self and subjectivity. It is not of minor coincidence that the dominate word of twenty-first century social networking is the "selfie." The great focal point of modern digital photography has become the fascinating subject of *Me*. Disregard the great landscape, architecture, or other amazing scenery, take a moment and ponder the greatness of "Me."

This degradation of culture was foretold in biblical prophecy. "But understand this, that in the last days there will come times of difficulty. For people will be lovers of self, lovers of money, proud, arrogant, abusive, disobedient to their parents, ungrateful, unholy" (1 Timothy 3:1–2). One may be curious as Paul's inclusion of the phrase in this text regarding disobedient children and its implied impact on society.

Psychotherapist and Holocaust survivor Viktor Frankl sheds light on the implications of college campuses being a petri dish of self-worship. Frankl emphasizes not only the error of teaching materialism and scientism as objective truth, but also the inherent danger. The result is a corruption of humanity through a flawed self-perception of being a mere product of instinct, heredity, and environment. The end-state of adoption of this thinking is nihilism.

> The gas chambers of Auschwitz were the ultimate consequence of the theory that man is nothing but the product of heredity and environment; or as the Nazi liked to say, "of Blood and Soil." I am absolutely convinced that the gas chambers of Auschwitz, Treblinka, and Maidanek were ultimately prepared not in some Ministry or other

in Berlin, but rather at the desks and lecture halls of nihilistic scientists and philosophers.[5]

The god of self may only be an intellectual construct of the twenty-first century, but it represents a real and metastasizing danger to our individual psychology, to our society, and to our future litmus test for truth. The non-theist groups posit a wide range of views, most contradictory, on self. For example, Sam Harris suggests self is just an illusion, but then disagrees with his mentor Daniel Dennett as he argues against the concept of free will.[6]

Many of the interview participants stated concerns that reflected moral judgement of the biblical God. One participant lamented, "How could God have not allowed me to pursue my dream?" At no point in the interview did the participant consider that God may have had a different, more meaningful, more fulfilling plan for his life. This is a symptom of the cultural pandemic of Me; one is unwilling to evaluate anything beyond what they *want*, certain in lieu of what they may *need*.

Many interview participants complained about religion "forcing them to believe" certain things that conflicted with their social or political perspectives. Me-centered thinking does not have God or objective truth at the top of its hierarchy. Subjective opinion, personal feelings, and instant gratification represent the triune godhead of postmodernism.

Truth does not change with the winds of culture. Truth is not defined by convenience. Truth is not defined by what is fashionable. Fourth-century Theologian and Philosopher Augustine of Hippo famously lamented, "I looked for pleasure, beauty, and truth, not in God but in myself and his other creatures, and the search led me instead to pain, confusion, and error."[7]

Psychologist Paul Vitz, in his 2010 work on *Psychology as Religion*,[8] maintains that modern psychology (in drawing a par-

---

5. Frankl, *Doctor and the Soul*, 27.
6. Harris, *Free Will*, 23.
7. Augustine, *Confessions*, 22–3.
8. Vitz, *Psychology as Religion*, 31.

allel to the concepts of scientism, atheism, humanism and related -*isms*) has become a religion in itself; a secular cult of self that has become part of the problem rather than part of the solution.

> The whole focus on our selves feeds unrealistic self-love, which psychologists often call "narcissism." One would have thought America had enough trouble with the narcissism of the "Me Generation" in the 1970s and with the Yuppies in the 1980s. But today's search for self-esteem is just the newest expression of America's tradition of egomania. The "feel good" created by such words (i.e., "You are the most important person in the whole world") is closer to a drug-induced high than any reality. It pacifies, seduces, distracts. It fills the empty self, but it perpetuates passivity and weakness.[9]

Author and pastor Rick Warren gives caution to this perspective with the very first sentence in his most famous work, *The Purpose Driven Life*:

> It's not about you. The purpose of your life is far greater than your own personal fulfillment, your peace of mind, or even your happiness. Its far greater than your family, your career, or even your wildest dreams or ambitions. If you want to know why you were placed on this planet, you must first begin with God. You were born *by* his purpose and *for* his purpose.[10]

What is the danger in focusing on self? The issue is perspective. It was not coincidental that Satan took Jesus to a mountain top during his temptation. Perspective changes when self is elevated; everything else looks small and insignificant in comparison to one's view at the moment. Conversely, to appreciate God's glory, one looks upward to the heavens (Psalms 19:1). When one looks at the night sky, one realizes the mammoth totality of creation—and how relatively insignificant they are in comparison.

The ultimate significance of this juxtaposition is not rooted purely in scale. It is based on the fact that regardless of how small

---

9. Vitz, *Psychology as Religion*, 32.
10. Warren, *The Purpose Driven Life*, 17.

one may seem, in reality, each human life is greatly consequential in the eyes of the Divine. However, to achieve greatness in this sense, one cannot focus on himself in the process. In yet another great dichotomy of Christian truth, humanity benefits more from focusing on God than focusing on themselves (Matthew 22:40).

The Christian apologist must confront this cultural dilemma and give voice to this great and inconvenient truth; *self* is the most inadequate god anyone could ever worship. The Gospel of Jesus Christ contains a solution to humanity's epic malady of inadequacy. The legitimate Christian life is defined by crucifixion of the self. In its place is a God truly worthy of worship. In making this transaction, a person can become more than capable of addressing the challenges of this world. Paul, in his letter to the church of Galatia proclaims, "I have been crucified with Christ. It is no longer I who live, but Christ who lives in me. And the life I now live in the flesh I live by faith in the Son of God, who loved me and gave Himself up for me" (Galatians 2:20).

There are two aspects of the atheist doctrine and tactics related to organized religion. The first is based on a political and societal assault to eliminate the freedom of organized religion as an element of modern society. For an ideology that claims a foundation in science, the basis for this doctrine seems once again, contradictory. There is ample scientific research on the psychological benefit of religion on human beings.[11]

There are only two conclusions one can draw from this fact: either the psychological and societal utility of religion has a transcendent source (i.e., from God) or it has a naturalist source (i.e., a survival-driven advancement of morality analysis influenced only by Darwinian evolution). Given those choices, the atheist ideology is either in direct conflict with the Creator-God or in direct conflict with clinical psychology. The atheist ideology is built upon a house of cards based on volitional blindness to a real, legitimate benefit for the human psyche.

---

11. Hackney and Sanders, "Religiosity and Mental Health;" Headey et al., "Authentic Happiness Theory;" Waite and Lehrer, "The Benefits from Marriage and Religion."

The second aspect of this atheist doctrine is the search for a replacement religion, although the atheist would certainly resist this characterization of the atheist doctrine. Augustine recognized the deep draw of the Divine. "You made us for yourself Lord: and our hearts are restless until they come to rest in you."[12] The atheist is aware of this yearning. It is a subconscious yearning to obtain righteousness. It is a subconscious yearning in search of redemption. Atheist John Gray explains:

> Contemporary atheism is a flight from a godless world. Life without any power that can secure order, or some kind of ultimate justice is frightening and for many an intolerable prospect. In the absence of such a power, human events could be finally chaotic, and no story could be told that satisfied the need for meaning. Struggling to escape this vision, atheists have looked for surrogates of the God they cast aside. The *progress of humanity* has replaced divine providence. But this faith in humanity makes sense only if it continues ways of thinking that have been inherited from monotheism. The idea that the human species realizes common goals throughout history is a secular avatar of a religious idea of redemption.[13]

A number of the participants in the research for this book mentioned that they attend Unitarian Universalist churches (UUC) in the area. Given this lead, an interview was scheduled with the leader of a local UUC to better understand how such an ideology attempts to determine truth amongst so many disparate faiths and why this form of "church" would be a draw for atheists.

The leader of the church was a self-described panentheist.[14] While the panentheist believes in spirituality, there were common elements between the UUC ideology and atheism, such as the moral, ethical, and intellectual adequacy of self. When I asked

---

12. Augustine, *Confessions*, 201.

13. Gray, *The Seven Types of Atheism*, 1.

14. "Panentheism" refers to a belief that rejects a personal deity but embraces the transcendent, claiming that god is in consciousness and in the universe itself. Alternatively, "Pantheism" suggests that the universe itself is a manifestation of God.

how he ministered to atheists in his church, he responded, "One ministry challenge of the UU church is to not move them from where they are today, but to get them comfortable with where they are today. Most people are good." When I pressed the issue on the UUC litmus test for *good* and *bad*, he admitted a lack of objective basis for the distinction; he struggled with contriving a subjective basis for morality as well.

Other contradictions of the Unitarian Universalist worldview included an embrace of the story of Jesus, albeit with a rejection of His historicity and certainly His divinity. The leader explained that most of his congregation would self-describe as "liberal Christians;" however, they espoused clearly non-biblical tenets outside of the realm of historical Christianity, such as homosexuality and so-called "social justice." He further stated that he condemns Christianity (as a formal religious institution) for being "dehumanizing" and "prejudiced," and declared theism itself to be "heretical."

He further explained the church's focus on love, acceptance, compassion, and empathy. He explained how he decided to allow a registered sex offender to attend the church and its social functions, albeit with specific rules prohibiting unsupervised access to non-adults. The sex offender proceeded to ignore the rule, was confronted, then proceeded to leave the congregation.

This story illustrates the dichotomous and contradictory ideology of the non-Christian. While claiming unconditional love for the sex offender, they still assume behavioral conditions and considerations for him. Still, in not being able to call out morality and ethical dilemmas, they have created a crisis from their approach and their assumptions on how to properly minister to people such as the sex offender.

Without a proper spiritual, mental, and psychological diagnosis, the patient is not cured (or even treated) and remains a threat to himself and to others. While some moral dilemmas do not reach the levels of societal threats, as the case with the sex offender, a lack of a moral and spiritual assessment yields similar results. As a result of this lack of moral prognosis and correlated treatment, the sex offender simply proceeded to act—yet again—on his instincts and unfettered innate desires.[15]

A person must realize he or she has a problem before they can move forward for proper curative treatment. Denying this assessment, then having that self-acceptance reinforced societally, simply results in an exacerbation of the problem. To simply declare oneself as adequate in their status quo, in virtually any aspect of life, the result will be either intellectual apathy, moral stagnation, or dangerous, willful blindness.

It seems there is no secular solution to the yearning of the soul of humanity. The snake oil options being pawned today are red herrings with a trail that ends in despair. The atheistic tenets of belief and disbelief are a house built on intellectual and moral shifting sand.

Atheists tend to apply more of a benign label to their belief system than is formally represented in their platforms. They tend to use "agnostic" more often than "atheist" and certainly more often than "anti-theist." There are also convoluted combination labels such as "gnostic atheists." Curiously, if one compares these relatively benign labels as descriptors of atheism with the official position statement of any local atheist organization, the tenets seem to shift from the benign (which provides something of a security blanket against burden of proof) and exposes their true focus, that being, outright anti-religion activism.

For example, below is the official *Position Statement* from the Charlotte Atheists and Agnostics organization. The statement begins with a declaration of "freedom of conscious" with equal consideration and "respect for all people." From there, the statement becomes much more aggressive:

> We oppose any laws or policies that seek to establish, promote, or prefer any religion in favor of any other religion or non-religion. We support the right of the individual to practice religion to the degree that such observance neither hampers nor violates the rights of others.

---

15. Hall, "Sexual Offender Recidivism," 802–9.

> We oppose the encroachment of religion into public education. We support an objective, fact-based public educational system with those facts supported by empirical evidence. We recognize the overwhelming scientific support for the theory of evolution and reject any proposal to include creationism, in any form, in a science classroom. We believe that all world beliefs, including creationism, are worthy of study in the proper educational context.[16]

The statement concludes with a declaration of support for abortion rights, LGBTQ+ rights, "marriage equality" and support for the right "of all consenting adults to conscientiously manage their own sexual behavior with no intrusions or limitations."[17]

The dichotomy of the non-threatening atheist propaganda against the backdrop of the hardcore atheist doctrine is either reflective of an inner conflict among the atheists and agnostics or a weak attempt to veil a clearly established system replacement religion, albeit one with a leftist social and political platform.

Since these beliefs lack any positive evidential support, while aggressively positioning different belief systems against each other politically, not just ideologically, the religion of modern atheism is a potentially dangerous kind. These statements reflect the clear dactylogram of activism, scientism, social bias, and certainly could be exemplified as the antithesis of free thinking and free speech.

In his book, *Seven Types of Atheism*, author John Gray disagrees with the modern atheistic propaganda and the ideology of the New Atheists. Gray considers modern atheism as nothing more than a "transmutation" of Christianity. He rejects the claim that culture or the human condition can be seen through a homogeneous interpretation. Gray is also against "progress" as defined by atheists as "an avatar of a religious idea of redemption."[18] Although progress is legitimate in science and technology, in his opinion negative aspects of humanity in the areas of ethics and

---

16. "Charlotte Atheists and Agnostics."
17. "Charlotte Atheists and Agnostics."
18. Gray, *The Seven Types of Atheism*, 1.

politics simply have new disguises. His most significant example is regarding imperialism, which "revives itself as a liberationist regime."[19]

Gray's third type of atheism is science itself. However, in Gray's perspective, "Human evolutionism, the illegitimate offspring of Darwinism, applied natural selection to the interpretation of human development." In essence, atheists replace one deity with another: the replacement being an idealistic, carbon-based specter of redemption and meaning.

> The God of monotheism did not die, it only left the scene for a while in order to reappear as humanity – the human species dressed up as a collective agent, pursuing its self-realization in history. But, like the God of monotheism, humanity is the work of the imagination. The only observable humanity is the multitudinous human animal, with its conflicting goals, values, and ways of life. As an object of worship, this fractious species has some disadvantages.[20]

Gray continues his attack on atheist tenets by questioning the faith in the concept of a human species as Marx's communal workers,[21] or Mill's autonomous individuals,[22] or Nietzsche's *Ubermench*.[23] "None of these fantastical creatures have been seen by human eyes. A truly human species remains as elusive as any deity. Humanity is the *deus absconditus* of modern atheism."[24]

Gray questions whether a truly freethinking atheist would challenge the prevailing faith in humanity, but he expressed doubt that there is any chance this community would give up their

---

19. Gray, *The Seven Types of Atheism*, 1.
20. Gray, *The Seven Types of Atheism*, 157.
21. Marx, *The Communist Manifesto, Part II*.
22. Individual autonomy is an idea that is generally understood to refer to the capacity to be one's own person, to live one's life according to reasons and motives that are taken as one's own and not the product of manipulative or distorting external forces, to be in this way independent. See Mill, *On Liberty*.
23. Nietszche, *Thus Spoke Zarathustra*.
24. Gray, *Seven Types of Atheism*, 156.

"reverence for this phantom." Gray suggests, "Without the faith that they stand at the head of an advancing species, they could hardly go on. Only by immersing themselves in such nonsense can they make sense of their lives. Without it, they face panic and despair."[25]

Gray's final assault of modern atheism in general (certainly the New Atheism in particular) is that the ideology is simply a continuation of monotheism; the difference being, the god who has dominion over the new monotheism is humanity itself.

> Hence, the unending succession of God-surrogates, such as humanity and science, technology, and the all-too-human vision of transhumanism. But there is no need for panic or despair. Belief and unbelief are poses [that] the mind adopts in the face of an unimaginable reality.[26]

The virtue framework of the apostate seems to be *moral relativism*, the antithesis of moral objectivity. Regardless of the note of legitimate intent in its counterintuitive label, moral relativism is chaos, which gives the false impression of order, influence, and ownership to the observer only because it establishes order in their own mind (locally). Still, it cannot extend beyond local (to universal) because everyone else is doing the same thing. The political left addresses this worldview "influence gap" by a fascist enforcement of groupthink[27] by eliminating free speech and establishing a common enemy (the political right in particular, or *anyone* who challenges their flawed philosophy, in general).[28]

If someone remains in the circle of groupthink, they are "safe" from attack. As a member of the group, the false impression of freedom from personal responsibility is also pandered. The group can attack any perceived encroachment on its moral boundary domain by claiming oppression and attempted theft of "freedom" of the group. The thought being, if the members of the group have a

---

25. Gray, *Seven Types of Atheism*, 157.
26. Gray, *Seven Types of Atheism*, 158.
27. Decision-making by a group, especially in a manner that discourages creativity and individual responsibility.
28. Hutson, "Why Liberals Aren't as Tolerant."

perceived personal benefit of the issue, the personal benefit overrides any challenge to the issue, including moral.

If one extends outside of that thought boundary, they are attacked and demonized not for only their worldview, but for their deviation from the group narrative. This is the tactic of so-called "social justice warriors" who claim a fight against racism by using racists tactics themselves, such as claims of white privilege; or a fight against oppression by using tactics of pure anarchy such as looting, murder, and other forms of blatant violence.[29]

The major problem for those who claim the Christian label but who espouse clearly non-biblical ideology, centers on biblical doctrine. A Christian is someone who gives lordship of their life to Jesus Christ and His truth, which is recorded in biblical Scripture. It is not theologically possible to reconcile the conflict between the sanctity of life, marriage, and biblical morality with modern social concepts embraced by the political left unless one works to skew the interpretation of the bible through a cultural lens. Leftist "Christians" rationalize this conflict by attempting to reduce biblical commands to a relativistic state, affixing the label of *fundamentalist* as a pejorative to modern biblical believers, and by challenging interpretation or applicability of the ancient text to today's "advanced society." This is particularly common among pro-gay religious scholars, as an example.[30]

The modern Christian must realize that the only way to use the Bible, recognized as the authoritative, transmitted Word of God, is as a lens to evaluate culture. If one breaks from teaching Scripture established by traditional doctrine and guided by the Holy Spirit, he or she is using culture as a lens to view the Bible (Colossians 2:8). This is the only way to justify ideas of moral relativity.

Jordan Peterson believes that we have lost this focus on the Bible and on Christ, whom Peterson argues is the archetypical ideal man and perfect source of objectives truths. This ultimately establishes Jesus as the basis of an ideal worldview. The "Word

---

29. White, "To Black Lives Matter, No Lives Matter."
30. Tillman, "Church's Response to Homosexuality," 243–60.

become flesh" is the substantiation of this truth (the Logos) with humanity so we can act out this worldview. This is the fundamental, historical, moral basis of western culture.

Peterson believes we will not survive without it, suggesting that while atheists and leftist suggest they are evidentialist regarding the state of the world today, they fail miserably in intellectually demonstrating a cohesive and positively influential structure to their ideology.

> Moral relativism may give personal satisfaction, but it does so at the destruction of society. This is what Nietzsche meant when he said, "God is dead, and we have killed him, and there will never be enough water to wash off the blood." He predicted that millions of people would die in the 20th century as a result of Communist ideology.[31]

Peterson further noted the loss of a strong moral cultural foundation, lamenting the fact that western society has come unmoored from truth and objectivity. "We oscillate from the radical right (hyper-order) to the radical left (hyper-chaos). We have nothing to keep us centered. What we need to keep us centered is the Logos. Whether they know it or not, it's the Logos."[32]

THE DECONVERTED REFLECT VULNERABILITY

There are four distinct categories of religious identity that reflect the nature and depth of religious commitment. For the purposes of this investigation, the four categories include:

The Churched (divided into two subgroups)
The Seeker
The Unchurched
The Nones

Among regular church attendees who self-describe as Christian, this research has identified two clear ideological subgroups.

---

31. "Heritage Discusses Socialism with Jordan Peterson."
32. "Heritage Discusses Socialism with Jordan Peterson."

These subgroups have different personal political and social perspectives, a tendency to interpret scripture differently, and a different level of appreciation for key tenets of Christian practice. These groups will be subcategorized religiously as 1) Conservative and 2) Liberal.

Figure 3 delineates the general profile of each group. Due to the thesis of this book, the attention will be drawn to the Church Liberal.

PROFILE				
The Church Conservative	The Church Liberal	The Seeker	The Unchurched	The Nones
Consistent across all ideological pillars (theological, political, sociological)	Inconsistent across religious, social, and political pillars	Evidence of reason, purpose, value, and meaning	Evidence of relevance	Strong theologically positive arguments and weak negative arguments
Strong theological presuppositions	Weak theological presuppositions	Theological and utility beliefs, seeking right spiritual "home"	Majority theist, but no belief in utility of religion	Generally anti-theistic beliefs
God-centric life purpose	Culture-centric life purpose with strong utility beliefs	God-centric life purpose with utility emphasis	Generally, culture-centric life purpose with no utility appropriation	Self-centric life purpose
Low risk of apostasy, unless experiential	Higher risk of apostasy, resentment of conservative grounding of biblical authority	Low risk of apostasy due to appreciation of "utility" of religion	Lower risk of apostasy but apathetic to religiosity due to perceived lack of relevance and low level of Christian resentment	Apostates or unbelievers

Figure 3

Among the theistic groups represented in Figure 3 (the Church Conservative, the Church Liberal, The Seeker, and The Unchurched) most of the Christian apostates in our research originated from the Church Liberal group. In examining the characteristics of this group, the Church Liberal has the ideological profile which suggests they are most vulnerable to a theological presuppositional shift. Among members of this group, as observed during the interviews, there is a distinct prioritization of culture over tenets of traditional Christianity. There is a perception that the concept of morality has evolved over time, relegating the moral framework of the past to the rubbish heap of the antiquated, the obsolete, and the intellectually inferior.

For example, modern social themes carry more weight with this group than does biblical authority, due to a perception that the evolution of cultural memes provides a more morally relevant foundation for the complexities of modern society than ideologies which have a long term historical and traditional basis, although admittedly relevant for their bygone time.

Knox's *Sacro-egoism* work describes this group accurately—one that he labels as Sacro-Egoists. Knox explains the evolution of theological thought in Western history, shifting from authority being recognized in the church and religious leaders (Sacro-Clericalism) to a basis of thought where the individual assumes the greatest authority (Sacro-Egoism).

The Sacro-Egoists (using Knox's nomenclature—a.k.a., the "Churched Liberal" as labeled above) have weak theological, biblical, and presuppositional foundations. Knox explains the basis of this ideological shift beginning in the nineteenth century:

> The role of the individual, the self, was elevated more than ever before and self-reliance was glamorized, epitomized, and utilized in society – even until the present. Liberal theologians sought to anchor their faith in common human experience and interpret it in ways that made sense in the modern worldview.[33]

This perspective not only tarries today but has been celebrated and advanced by the liberal wing of the twenty first century Christian church due to their embrace of social trends and memes.

Regardless of the desire for community, purpose, and meaning interpreted by the church, the top of the Sacro-egoist personal hierarchy of values is *self*, which explains why they find such intellectual comfort in the confines of liberal/leftist political ideology—an ideology also based on *self*, certainly not on the transcendent, and certainly not on Christ. Thus, their cognitive dissonance is genuine, uncomfortable, and seeks resolution.

For these people, resolution of their dissonance is as simple as a presuppositional shift away from God as a reality in the universe.

---

33. Knox, *Sacro-Egoism*, 23.

All internal ideological tension vanishes in this single decision; or so they claim. In the trade-off,[34] they gain the acceptance of postmodern culture, of the broadcast media, of the university, of the music industry, of the Hollywood elite, of social media, of the prevailing thought in corporate America, and of the loudest and most aggressive antagonists in society.

One key point of tension that the former Christians experienced is centered on the claim that objective morality only exists if God exists. From a secular socio-political perspective, Psychologist Jonathan Haidt provides further clarity on the distinctive personal perspectives on the concept of morality, or to be specific, on the judgement between "right" and "wrong."[35] In his research (which corresponds with the interview assessments detailed in this book), there was a distinctive difference of values between politically liberal and politically conservative participants. The liberal participants placed a higher value on foundations of care and fairness, with greater rejection of foundations of loyalty, authority, and sanctity. Conservative research participants had a similar level of appreciation for care and fairness, but also respected the foundations of loyalty, authority, and sanctity.

The socio-theological conclusion is that the politically conservative Christian will be less vulnerable to societal and cultural winds of change because Christianity, the Bible, and the role of the corporate church has value, meaning, and purpose as a stable and respected foundation of objective morality in their lives. However, the politically liberal Christian provides intellectually fertile soil for the seeds of cultural propaganda wrapped in the appearance of morality and ethics, regardless of the reality of its evil substrate.

Theologically, for the Christian deconvert, the trade-off is much more dire and grim. They seem to favor trading the transcendent for the material and the relevant—the immediate satisfaction of a syringe filled with false hope and meaning due to its immediate "high" of subjective truth and perceived relevance.

---

34. Cameron, *Experiences and Meanings of Adults*, 132.
35. Haidt, *The Righteous Mind*, 183–84.

Sadly (or ironically), they do not immediately recognize the side effects from the conversion.

It is apparent that the Christian deconverts feel that they only lose Jesus, a character in a collection of children's fables. They only lose a promise from antiquity. They only lose a basis of wishful thinking. They only lose a belief in something unseen. They only lose an outdated and error-filled book. They only lose a reputation of being judgmental and hypocritical. So, why not make the shift? The gain is perceived much greater than the loss and consequently, their cognitive dissonance dissolves. However, it is apparent that even they sense that something else is askew – and a difference sort of cognitive dissonance is borne.

They may be angry at the church, or at Christians, or at God Himself, but there is something regarding humanity's inner search for righteousness that drives them to seek it elsewhere. The Bible speaks of this explicitly as humanity anxiously attempting to flee the spirit of God (Ephesians 2:10, Psalm 139:7–8). Psychologists are now finding evidence where the brain seems hard-wired for this search and even reacts differently once religious thoughts are embraced.[36] Of course, atheists do not acknowledge this inner yearning as a search for God; however, it is apparent from this research that the inner voice never ceases to summon, in spite of intellectual rejection.

Most of the participants in this research recognized some aspects of the utility of religion. Psychologist Malcolm Paul Cameron based his doctoral thesis on the topic of deconversion for the University of British Columbia's Psychology department. Regarding the participants retrospective on fundamentalist Christianity, the deconverts acknowledged a certain emotional and relational appeal which addressed the natural longings of human beings. Its attraction includes the fact that the offer of community extends to those already converted, in the process of converting, as well as to non-converted seekers.

---

36. Muller, "Are We Hard-Wired for God?"

Evangelical fundamentalism appeals to people because of its built-in 'family oriented' and welcoming presence grounded in the belief that people are special, that they are persons of worth and significance due to being created in the image of God, that they matter to the Christian community at large, that God has a special plan of their lives, and that their purposes here on earth can be more easily recognized, understood, and acted out in the context of knowing God while being a part of His special people who do His special work. Evangelical fundamentalism places great emphasis on the traditional nuclear family and opposes anything that might be a threat to maintaining this particular model and approach to faith and life.

Ideological alternatives to Christianity, certainly non-theistic alternatives, engage in a continual pursuit of relativistic principles that form a construct of ethics, attempting to identify or balance the "best" of ideologies which may even outright contradict on certain levels. The doctrine of the Universalist Unitarian church is an example of such an entanglement of ideals. This religion is simultaneously a religion of all religions and a religion of no religion. They state no formal creed but believe there is some truth in all religions. They claim a "free and responsible search for truth and meaning;" yet, they make no formal stance on the definition, source, or basis of such truth.

The apostle Paul describes the balancing of disparate ideologies as one carrying around a dead carcass (Romans 7: 24).[37] Those people must find redemption elsewhere if they do not accept it from Christ and the only way to accept Christ's redemption is to lay down the burden of the dead carcass of *self* (Matthew 16:24).

While interviewees used the words, "peace" and "freedom," in describing their post-deconversion mindset, it was unclear if that sentiment reflected reality or their aspiration. Some comments suggested the latter. One apostate said she now fears death,

---

37. The penalty for murder in the ancient Middle East included being forced to carry around the victim's dead body during a time prior to prison. Virgil, *The Aeneid of Virgil*, 483–88.

whereas she never did before. Two people broke down crying during our interview as they discussed their deconversion. One person stated that they missed the sense of confidence about the hereafter that they enjoyed as a Christian. Many were angry. A few were despondent. All were obviously deeply affected by their transition.

Author and Psychologist John S. Brent suggests the post-deconversion psychological trauma can sometimes become clinically significant.[38] The twenty-first century Christian church must understand that there are individuals experiencing such psychological conflict in their congregation today. They sit in the same pews alongside members of twenty years. They may themselves be members of twenty years. There are several questions that the modern Christian church must ask in dealing with the impact of postmodern culture on the church body.

Should apologetics be at the core of the church curriculum for discipleship training?

During Christ's temptation (Mathew 4:1-11; Luke 4:1–13), Satan explicitly attacked three fundamental weaknesses of the human character. These can be general characterized as Hedonism (the pursuit of pleasure or self-indulgence—i.e., "Stones to be made into bread"); materialism (material possessions and physical comfort is more important than spiritual values—i.e. "All these things I will give you"); and egoism (self-interest is the foundation of morality—i.e., "Throw yourself down . . . and on their hands they will bear you up").

The enemy of Christ is using these same intellectual lures today. There was not a single exception of the research participants who did not claim one, if not all, of these concepts as being at the top of their new hierarchy of values. The act of eliminating God from their belief system was characterized as "eliminating

---

38. Brent, "Leaving Protestant Fundamentalism," 205–14.

hypocrisy," "adding more peace," and "eliminating judgment" from their lives as a result.

Ultimately, for the deconverted Christian, the deal was accepted. Their souls were traded for "pleasure" to be glorified, for "power" to be obtained, and for "proof" that indeed, they are "god." Christ's response to these lies is as important today as it was 2000 years. Truth is found only in God (Matthew 4:4; Luke 4:4). People need to trust God (Matthew 4:7; Luke 4:12). People need to serve God (Matthew 4:10; Luke 4:8). These three elements define the primary directive and presuppositions of the followers of Jesus Christ.

In leveraging Christ's example, the church's primary learning from this research is regarding the vital importance of prioritizing presuppositional apologetics in discipleship and outreach. Christ is the center of our system of belief, but if there is no God, there is no Father, there is no Son, and there is no Savior. Not one of the research participants questioned the existence of Jesus, but all of them, post deconversion, questioned the existence of God. Many of them had done so for years, even during the time they claimed the label of "Christian."

The modern church member is bombarded with anti-religious opinions, accusations, and outright lies about virtually every aspect of the Christian worldview. Church leadership must recognize the depth of this spiritual warfare and become more devoted to an aggressive plan to inform, empower, and equip the parishioner. Comprehensive apologetics in defense of transcendent presuppositions, the Bible, and the Resurrection must be prioritized.

How much of the church's schedule and budget goes toward community outreach?

Among atheists and those who have renounced their faith, the church is seen as a leader in dispensing propaganda but not a leader in demonstrating Christ's involvement with society. Many of the interviewees joined atheist organizations after their deconversions specifically as an outlet for their secular altruism. One deconvert who is an officer in a local atheist organization explained:

> Losing my mother (death due to illness) lit a fire under me to be a better person. If she was going to live on, I decided it must be through my life. I decided that I needed to be more charitable and compassionate. Even as a Christian, I wasn't doing it as much as my mom. I am trying to make up for her being gone. I sought out an atheist group for community service options which were not Christian based. Everything I had seen was based on Christianity.

"Charitable" and "compassionate" are normally words associated with Christianity; yet this interview participant associated them with atheistic community outreach. The atheist community has established this strategy as a legitimate route for the atheist to prove that although they do not recognize the existence of God, this tangible expression of compassion proves they are not inherently evil but are in fact "good" people. Certainly, apostates are attempting to find an alternative path to personal redemption through this action, but regardless of the motivation, this is not an area where the church should be perceived as reluctant leaders.

According to a study by the Evangelical Christian Credit Union, most of the average church budget (>85%) is on payroll, administration, and facilities. Some 3% (regardless of size) is spent on children's programs, 2% on adult programs, and only 1% is spent on local, national, and international benevolence.[39] This does not reflect an intense commitment for the church to be a visible and active contributor to the community. In this battle, the atheist's strategy may have any opportunity to "walk the walk" of concern for society while the perception of the church is that it only "talks the talk."

---

39. "2013 Church Budget Allocations."

Is the Gospel being diluted to be more palatable to culture?

The Apostle Paul was determined to keep his message in rigid synchronization with the same Gospel being preached by the original disciples (Galatians 1:11–2:10). Paul wanted to make sure that his own memory, intellect, perspective, or the influence of culture would not adulterate the truth of Jesus that he was preaching. There is little evidence to support a similar concern in the pulpit of the average Christian church in America today.

Most churches are in survival mode today due to the financial overhead of keeping the doors open. Some 85% of churches in America today have less than 100 congregants and few have ever spiked to 200.[40] This forces pastors at these churches to be bivocational, simply to provide for their family. As a result, church growth is a priority for purposes of fiscal survival. There is certainly ample motivation to preach to accommodate "itching ears" (2 Timothy 4:3) if one risks alienating half of congregants for political reasons and other congregants of self-professing "Christians" who question the authority of Scripture, certainly as it applies to polemical topics in modern society.

There is motivation to soften the "sales-pitch," to sound more seeker-sensitive and preach a feel-good gospel of prosperity. This strategy tries to focus on God only, because Christ is too controversial. It cuts out the Old Testament because it is too tough to defend apologetically and besides, the God of the Old Testament is mean and angry.[41] Instead, they strive to adopt the framework of social justice; it places the church in the good graces of the postmodernists. The concept of "sin" is a prohibited topic; modern society suggests one should kindly embrace one's current self—as is.

A young pastor would be tempted to follow this formula to have a decent chance to grow their church and increase the coffers; but that is not what Christian leaders are called to do. In what is

---

40. Bird and Carl, *How to Break the 200 Barrier*, 115.
41. "Beyond the Commandments."

seen as an exhortation to every minister of the Gospel of Jesus Christ, Paul proclaims to Timothy:

> I charge you in the presence of God and of Christ Jesus, who is to judge the living and the dead, and by his appearing and his kingdom. Preach the word; be ready in season and out of season; reprove, rebuke, and exhort, with complete patience and teaching.
>
> For the time is coming when people will not endure sound teaching but having itching ears, they will accumulate for themselves teachers to suit their own passions and will turn away from listening to the truth and wander off into myths. As for you, always be sober-minded, endure suffering, do the work of an evangelist, fulfill your ministry.

This is the Gospel of Jesus Christ, as stated in I Corinthians 15; Christ defeated death in remission for our sins. If the church does not preach Jesus, the church is not preaching the Gospel. If the church does not preach the resurrection, the need for humanity's remission of sin, or the Divinity of Christ, the church is not preaching the Gospel. As a result of Jesus's divinity, His word is true. Jesus considered Scripture as being the Word of God. If the church does not preach the authenticity of Scripture, the church is not preaching the Gospel.

If the Bible is the Word of God, then the commands and directives included therein are directly inspired by God. Those commands include honoring the sanctity of life (Jeremiah 1:5; Psalm 139:13–16; Matthew 5:21–22), marriage as solely being between a man and a women (Genesis 1:27, 28; Mark 10:6–9; Ephesians 5:28, 33; Hebrews 13:4), salvation by faith and God alone (Ephesians 2:8–9; Galatians 2:16; Romans 3:28), love for your fellow man (John 15:12; 1 John 4:20; 1 Peter 2:17), and keeping Christ as the center of your life (Proverbs 3:5-6; Galatians 2:20; Philippians 1:20–21).

These commands and directives are inconvenient truths to modern society but this an example of the Bible being sharper than a two-edged sword, penetrating the joints and marrow, judging the thoughts and attitudes of the heart of humanity (Hebrews 4:12). Regardless of the changing winds of society, the leftist influence on culture, or the inconvenience of the message not being acceptable to itching ears, if the church preaches anything short of, exclusive of, or some variation of the above, the church is not preaching the legitimate Gospel of Jesus Christ.

Evangelist Leonard Ravenhill explains:

> Someone now warns us lest we become so heavenly minded that we are of no earthly use. Brother, this generation of believers is not, by and large, suffering from such a complex. The brutal, soul-shaking truth is that we are so earthly minded that we are of no heavenly use.
>
> In this hour, when the average church knows more about promotion than prayer, has forgotten consecration by fostering competition, and has substituted propaganda for propagation.[42]

In the spiritual warfare against the modern church, the Christian is leaving their main weapons in the barracks. Prayer is devalued across all segments of church membership. If it is reducing in frequency; it is certainly reducing in benefit and influence. Prayer is the vehicle to directly commune with Him (Philippians 4:6–7; James 5:6; Matthew 21:22; Romans 12:12). If God is God and people truly recognize this fact, the church must reestablish the priority of prayer. Ravenhill continues:

> No man is greater than his prayer life. The pastor who is not praying is playing; the people who are not praying are straying. We have many organizers, but few agonizers; many players and payers, few prayers; many singers, few clingers; lots of pastors, few wrestlers; many fears, few tears; much fashion, little passion; many interferers, few intercessors; many writers, but few fighters. Failing here, we fail everywhere.[43]

The church has lost its understanding of the power of prayer because the church has lost its expectation of supernatural

---

42. Ravenhill, *Why Revival Tarries*, 30.
43. Ravenhill, *Why Revival Tarries*, 25.

intervention by God. The claim of the godless is that unless God answers every prayer, exactly how people ask for it, in the time that people expect it, then He either does not care or He does not exist. While the unbeliever denies the power and the benefit, the church has no excuse and must reestablish this path to God. The greatest tool the Christian church has in this age of spiritual warfare is the power of prayer.

Does your church view Scripture through the lens of culture – or culture through the lens of Scripture?

My research on this question centered around an ideology which we revisit—a variant philosophical theory that is based on so-called "social justice" that has crept its way onto the radar of the modern Christian worldview—critical race theory (CRT). As previously explained, this theory suggests institutions are inherently racist, and that race is a socially constructed concept that is used by White people to further their economic and political interests at the expense of people of color. It is grounded in Marxism, a theory which suggests all of society should be categorized either as oppressed (minorities) or oppressors (Caucasians). While obvious to most Christians who view culture through the lens of the biblical mandate to love your neighbor as yourself (Mark 12:31), even to the casual observer, it is surprising how a divisive ideology could be taken seriously. Unfortunately, there is proof that it is not only pervasive, but also uncomfortably entrenched.

    I interviewed Kyle Whitt, a church planter formerly partnering with the North American Mission Board (NAMB), a domestic missions agency of the Southern Baptist Convention. Over the course of applications, assessments, conversations, and trainings to partner with and gain support from NAMB for his planting effort in the state of Washington, Whitt became very uncomfortable with the apparent ideological shift in the material and the message of NAMB that was developed for the purpose of establishing and growing new SBC churches. From his perspective, the message of the Christian Gospel was adulterated with a clear influence of language devoted to plant seeds of "social justice" and CRT, instead of a pure biblical interpretation of the Gospel.

I asked whether this infiltration reflected a substantive cultural perspective or whether this was actually a symptom of a broader church illness; that being, an expected embrace of alternative ideology for anyone who diverts from biblical authority:

> It is completely a cancer within the church. We saw waves of attacks against the church through the 19th and 20th century. CRT and "social justice" represent a new wave of attack over the past decade. In response to the liberal push in the 70s and 80s, there was an obvious correlated deviation from biblical inerrancy. In reaction (within the SBC), the majority steps forward and responded with an aggressive rejection of this threat with what is now referred to as "the conservative resurgence." The liberal cultural drift was defeated, as was its influence on the church. The problem was, they weren't driven out; they were just driven underground. Over time, we saw a liberal re-awakening. The "woke church", intersectionality, CRT, and related concepts slowly took root and those who did not research the concepts adequately were influenced because of the surface level propaganda.[44]

That propaganda, Whitt suggests, includes concepts that on the surface are clearly biblical principles: the defeat of injustice, feeding of the hungry, showing the love of Christ to the less fortunate, and so on. However, these divisive ideologies hijacked the words, *justice*, to mean *retaliation* and *retribution*. They established their own method of redemption (doing the work of racial penance and reconciliation), and seek to apply the Marxist-based, perpetual cycle of class and racial division onto society.

In essence, CRT and social justice is a new religion. Whitt continues:

> The twenty-first century Christian church has created a form of "nominal Christianity." People truly have no idea what they believe. This lack of proper grounding in

---

44. Whitt, interview by the author.

core Christian principles allowed a push of the liberal agenda from the bottom up. In the past, cultural Marxism was unable to gain a mainstream foothold in society or the church. Once the cancer metastasized in the past couple of decades, we saw massive shifts. We developed a generation that was ready to wholesale internalize these ideologies to the point where liberal leadership could actively talk about them. Take the near overnight shift in topics of sexuality and sexual biology as an example. In the church, our spiritual enemy hit us with biological warfare and slowly degraded the innate sense of biblical discernment so he could hit us with the kill shot of an alternative gospel. This influence was clearly seen in the materials, the ideology, and the mission drift of the North American Mission Board.[45]

CRT forces all people groups to take a side on the racial spectrum; if you are not actively supporting CRT and social justice, you are an enabler and therefore, an oppressor. It is imperative that the Christian church recognize this tactic. The instinct for someone rejecting this flawed ideology is to overreact and declare that these proponents of this flawed ideology are themselves evil. The Christian church must reject this instinct.

Our warfare is on a spiritual level and our enemy is the source this attack. To fight against this ideology by demonizing Blacks and liberal Whites is in itself, not based on biblical principles. The ideology must be rejected because of its divisiveness, assault on biblical principles, and its resonate hatefulness. However, the Christian church must understand how to reject such radical ideologies, while maintaining a biblical commitment to fight true injustice, and not just a politicized, hijacked definition. Christ's mandate to love one another as yourself is not stratified by race or ideology. We can love those we disagree with, without embracing hatred.

Love does not mandate intellectual capitulation of ungodly doctrine. Until the Christian church is able to master this realm of discernment, radical ideologies will continue to attempt to take

---

45. Whitt, interview by the author.

root in various forms of spiritual assault. The Christian church cannot teach and disciple truth if it cannot distinguish the legitimate Gospel from weak, flawed, destructive, self-centered, lawless propaganda.

6

Conclusion

THERE IS EVIDENCE OF the societal utility of Christianity, void of its transcendent substructure, having substantive and recognizable benefit. It provides a hyperlinked text written record to explain and defend objective truth, a historical record of positive influence on society, a collection of inspiring poetic literature, a psychologically impactful toolset, and a life-altering message of hope, meaning, and moral redemption—all while providing a framework for cross-cultural interpretation and adoption. There is nothing among the non-theistic worldviews that has any sort of potential for a similar universal impact or influence. Islam has grown via intimidation and threat of death for apostasy. Christianity grew despite threat of death. However, stripping Christianity of its divine authorship is not even a reasonable intellectual table-top exercise.

The power of Christianity is based solely on the divine authorship and divine authority. If Jesus Christ is not the Son of God and if He was not bodily resurrected, then the Christian faith is in vain (1 Corinthians 15:14). Christianity is particularly unique regarding its powerful collective basis of claims, evidence, and influence. Still, it has often been the most falsifiable or corrupted system in history by non-believers.

Only God can give relevance to truth for a creation separated by distance, culture, ideology, and experiences. Humanity can only establish a subjective version of truth, driven by our limited perspectives from our unique corner of the physical and intellectual world; but that source of truth, that God, is feeble and proven inadequate. Humanity can only establish a god in its own image—a god shown throughout history to be severely immoral, unscalable, unreliable, minimally influential, and finite. Only through willful blindness would one grant deity to such a flawed fantasy.

The atheist is not simply ambivalent to the concept of Christianity; they are angry and fearful. However, they struggle in explaining why fear a simple phantom. They claim God is a myth but still rail against Him, personally. While the atheists argue vehemently about the definitional variations of the brands of atheism, agnosticism, and anti-theism, after comparing their new worldview and beliefs from our research, there is little separation in the ideological basis of the three labels. Atheists and their ideological cousins do not just reject God; they despise the idea of God. One wonders why.

If God exists, then humanity is accountable. If God exists, then objective morality exists. If God exists, then the atheist, as the rest of humanity, is culpable. The atheist has no evidence against God; they simply hate the implications of His existence. The only way they know to escape the truth is to suppress it. While they reject the prospect of life having true meaning, they are now committed to experience what it feels like to have none.

The Christian deconvert renounces their religious faith and their recognition of God; yet evidence suggests they are threatened by what they now label as a fairytale. They attack what they once embraced. They impugn what they once revered, regardless of the fact that they have no positive proof for their new religion—and certainly no positive proof of its authority.

From the interview responses and the meta-analysis of scholarly research on this topic, the reason becomes evident; the atheists have a reason to hate God. One cannot establish objective

Conclusion

morality without God.[1] One cannot ground the concepts of good and evil without God. And one cannot escape accountability from God. They exist as a creature of His creation in a universe of His creation with a purpose of His creation; that being, to develop a personal relationship with them. They mistakenly believe they can escape His providence much in the way one believes he can escape their own shadow on a bright sunny day. They cannot escape it, at least in this realm, nor disprove the truth, and as a result, the best they can do is to hate it.

There are great questions for humanity for which atheists are not only incapable—but also unwilling—to provide an answer. What is meaning? What is purpose? Who is God? The Roman Governor Pontius Pilate met with Jesus to better understand why the Jewish leaders wanted him to be prosecuted (John 18: 38). Pilate ended their dialogue with the same question: "What is truth?" Humanity continues to ask this question two thousand years later.

The atheist attempts to avoid these questions because they are fearful of the answers. They pretend these abstract concepts are not relevant, but that perspective simply reflects intellectual laziness. Where would science be today if it were not for the early pioneers of the discipline being motivated to find answers to those questions? They suggest science can answers these questions, but that statement goes against the very definition of the scientific process. Besides, as God has written the moral law on our hearts, He has also embedded a yearning to those questions.

This research has demonstrated that the Christian deconvert is more devoted to anger at God than they are prepared to litigate His presence. Given the lack of evidence, in which they claim intellectual asylum in suggesting they have no burden of evidence, they fall back to a line of defense of why God is immoral and not worthy of worship. The inescapable conclusion is this: if God exists, humanity is accountable for their life choices. If God does not exist, we are our own god.

As terrifying as this premise may be, it is complicated by the fact that we have judged ourselves to be fine, despite our fatal

1. Koukl, *Tactics*, 160.

flaws.. If atheism is true, morality is not a topic for expansion, for maturation, or for exploration. If atheism is true, humanity's flawed perspective of relationship, of self, of sexuality, of morality, of purpose, of meaning, is simply fine the way it is. We push for progress in every academic area except the study of morality. From a moral perspective, the culture suggests stagnation is desirable, healthier, and kinder. Murder the unborn, silence those that disagree with you, and the ultimate measure of truth is if one "feels" good about it.

We love truth when it flatters us. We hate truth when it exposes us. Morality is a condition tied to truth. It is a tool solely designed for the advanced study of Self. It is a mirror, not a microscope. For the non-Christian, it offers an inconvenient truth that all attempt to escape, but they find no amnesty or benefit.

The Christian deconvert attempts to feign escape by challenging God's existence, yet they, in their hearts, know this is fallacy; therefore, they remain threatened. They then try to assault God's character, but they lack a sword that is sufficiently forged with an ability to divide good and evil. On what basis do we define those parameters and more importantly, if God fails that test, how does humanity possibly survive that degree of evaluation?

The learning from this research is not limited to the apostate. Today's church wants to be raptured from responsibility. It is the same with modern culture. We are in search of a religion and a god who serves *us*; and in finding that God, we can be relived of accountability and responsibility. Satan is selling the same hollow deal that he offered to Jesus Christ two thousand years ago. A person can become God. There are eager buyers of this snake oil in the streets of twenty-first century society—and shockingly, there are eager buyers of this snake oil in the pews of the twenty-first century church.

There is a reason why the research suggests that theself-described liberal Christian is experiencing cognitive dissonance. As a result of their philosophical struggle, they become prime candidates for deconversion. It is not possible to find God via a litmus test of social, political, and subjective moral viewpoints. Such an

Conclusion

attempt is simply a search for validation and confirmation by the creation—a creation which has limited insight, limited foresight, and a monumentally insufficient litmus test for truth, certainly based on a flawed and skewed interpretation of subjective morality.

True, historic, biblical Christianity insists that truth is based solely in the reality of Jesus Christ. If Jesus Christ existed and demonstrated authority over the natural world through His resurrection from the dead, as He predicted, He has all the reliability necessary to defend that premise. Only by starting with the recognition of this fact can one have the proper litmus test for truth for all things in your world. That recognition starts by recognizing—as valuable—the things that Christ says are valuable, including the Holy Scriptures.

Scripture carries the authority of the word of God for one reason: because Christ says it does. A rejection of biblical Scripture is an early stage of a rejection of Christ and objective truth. In self-defining oneself as a liberal Christian, one is claiming a new religion, because in doing so, one must reject biblical authority and the authority of Christ. The conclusion of that re-prioritization is replacement of the deity at the top of one's hierarchy of values with themselves. This is not Christianity.

The toughest challenge for the modern apologist may indeed be the deconverted Christian, but that reality need not be intimidating. The Christian apologist is the messenger, not the Redeemer; the follower of Christ is an extension of life and light in the midst of darkness, not the Life-giver.

As Christians mature in the spiritual discipline of giving reason for the faith, they must keep one fact in mind: the greatest apologetic for any tough theological challenge is not purely grounded in persuasive argument, but rather, it is grounded in how effectively and sincerely Jesus Christ is exalted and essential in our own lives.

Appendix A

Deconversion Interview Questions

1. Demographics (first name, age group, race, Christian denomination, political ideology)

2. Did your de-conversion change/affect your political ideology?

3. How would you characterize the depth of your religious faith?

4. How would you characterize the depth of your current beliefs?

5. How would you characterize your belief in religious dogma? (biblical inerrancy, Jesus resurrection, bible prophecy, objective morality, etc.)

6. Of the three common definitions of non-theism, to which segment would you self-categorize? (atheist, agnostic, anti-theist)

7. What was the catalyst for your deconversion?

8. Are you better off or worse off because of your previous Christian faith? If you had to live your life over again, would you choose to have been an atheist your entire life?

9. What do you wish Christians better understood about atheism?

10. What do you miss the most about your Christian belief system or identity?

11. Which argument for Christianity was the toughest to defend?

Appendix A

12. What is the most positive aspect of your shift toward atheism?

13. Why did you feel it necessary to join a community of atheists?

14. If I was on the cusp on deconversion, but had yet to decide, what would you tell me to encourage me to take the final step?

15. If you could change one thing in the world today, what would it be? Also, what is your greatest fear?

Bibliography

Adam, R. J. "Leaving the Fold: Apostasy from Fundamentalism and the Direction of Religious Development." *Australian Religion Studies Review* 22 (2018) 42–63.

Adler, Mortimer. *Great Books of the Western World.* Chicago: Encyclopedia Britannica, 1952.

Augustine. *Confessions.* Oxford: Oxford Paperbacks, 1998.

Bahnsen, Greg L. *Presuppositional Apologetics: Stated and Defended.* Powder Springs: American Vision, 2008.

Babinski, E. *Leaving the Fold: Testimonies of Former Fundamentalists.* New York: Prometheus Books, 1995.

Barr, William. "Address on Religious Liberty." *American Rhetoric,* October 11, 2019. https://www.americanrhetoric.com/speeches/williambarrnotredame.htm.

Benn, Alfred W. "The Morals of an Immoralist-Friedrich Nietzsche. I." *International Journal of Ethics* 19.1 (1908) 1–23.

Berlinski, David. *The Devil's Delusion.* New York: Basic Books, 2011.

Bird, Warren and George Carl. *How to Break the 200 Barrier.* Grand Rapids: Baker, 1993.

Brent, J. S. "Leaving Protestant Fundamentalism: A Qualitative Analysis of a Major Life Transition." *Counseling and Values* 38 (1994) 205–14.

Bromley, D. G. *The Politics of religious Apostasy: The Role of Apostates in the Transformation of Religious Movements.* Connecticut: Greenwood, 1998.

Bruce, Steve. *God Is Dead: Secularization in the West.* Malden: Blackwell, 2002.

Bush, Daniel. "Religious Liberals Want to Change What it Means to be a Religious Voter." *PBS News Hour,* July 8, 2019. https://www.pbs.org/newshour/politics/religious-liberals-want-to-change-what-it-means-to-be-a-christian-voter.

Cameron, Malcom Paul. "The Experiences and Meanings of Adults Who Were Raised in and Later Departed From Evangelical Fundamentalism: A Descriptive Phenomenological Inquiry" (Master's Unpublished Thesis, University of British Columbia, 2008). https://open.library.ubc.ca/media/download/pdf/24/1.0054087/1

Bibliography

Cammaerts, Emile. *The Laughing Prophet: The Seven Virtues and G.K. Chesterton*. North Yorkshire: Methuen, 1937.

Charlotte Atheists and Agnostics. charlotteathesistorg.com. https://www.charlotteatheists.org/about-caa/position-statements.

Chesterton, G. K. *St. Thomas Aquinas*. New York: Random House, 1974.

Christian Century. "Beyond the Commandments: We Should Be Wary of Attempts to Unhitch the Ten Commandments from Their Religious Moorings." *The Christian Century*, May 3, 2005. https://www.christiancentury.org/article/2005-05/beyond-commandments.

Craig, William Lane. *On-Guard*. Colorado Springs: Cook, 2010.

———. *Reasonable Faith*. Wheaton: Crossway, 2008.

Cragun, R. T., and J. H. Hammer. "One Person's Apostate is Another Person's Convert: What Terminology Tells Us About Pro-Religious Hegemony in the Sociology of Religion." *Humanity & Society* 35 (2011) 149–75.

Creswell, J. W., W. E. Hanson, V. L. C. Plano, and A. Morales. "Qualitative Research Designs Selection and Implementation." *The Counseling Psychologist* 35 (2007) 236–64.

Copan, Paul. *Is God a Moral Monster?* Grand Rapids: BakerBooks, 2011.

Curry, Tom. "Critical Race Theory." *Encyclopedia Britannica*. https://www.britannica.com/topic/critical-race-theory.

Dagneau, Isaac. "Deconversion and Liberal Theology." *InDoubt*, July 23, 2018. https://www.indoubt.com/indoubt/episode-132-deconversion-and-liberal-theology/.

Dawkins, Richard. *A River out of Eden: A Darwinian View of Life*. New York: Basic Books, 1995.

———. *The God Delusion*. Boston: Houghton Mifflin, 2008.

Dennett, Daniel. "The Nefarious Neurosurgeon." *bigthink.com*. https://bigthink.com/videos/daniel-dennett-on-the-nefarious-neurosurgeon.

Dervic, Kanita, et al. "Religious Affiliation and Suicide Attempt." *American Journal of Psychiatry* 161.12 (2004) 2303–08.

D'Souza, Dinesh. *The Big Lie*. Washington: Regnery, 2017.

Dueck, Ryan. "Angry at the God Who Isn't There: The New Atheism as Theodicy." *Direction*, March 2011. https://directionjournal.org/40/1/angry-at-god-who-isnt-there-new-atheism.html.

Duignan, B. "Postmodernism." *Encyclopedia Britannica*. https://www.britannica.com/topic/postmodernism-philosophy.

ECCU. "2013 Church Budget Allocations, Learning Priorities, and Quarterly Financial Trends." *eccu.org*. http://web.archive.org/web/20141019033209/https://www.eccu.org/resources/advisorypanel/2013/surveyreports20.

Ehrman, Bart. *Jesus: Apocalyptic Prophet of the New Millennium*. New York: Oxford Press, 1999.

Ellens, J. Harold. "That Tough Guy from Nazareth: A Psychological Assessment of Jesus." *HTS Teologiese Studies / Theological Studies* 70.1 (2014) 1–8.

BIBLIOGRAPHY

Flew, Antony. *There is a God: How the World's Most Notorious Atheist Changed his Mind.* New York: HarperOne, 2007.

Frankl, Viktor. *The Doctor and the Soul: From Psychotherapy to Logotherapy.* New York: Vintage, 1986.

Gray, John. *The Seven Types of Atheism.* New York: Picador, 2018.

Hackney, C. H., and G. S. Sanders. "Religiosity and Mental Health: A Meta-Analysis of Recent Studies." *Journal for the Scientific Study of Religion* 42 (2003) 43–55. doi:10.1111/1468-5906.t01-1-00160.

Haidt, Jonathan. *The Righteous Mind.* New York: Vintage Books, 2012.

Hall, G. "Sexual Offender Recidivism Revisited: A Meta-Analysis of Recent Treatment Studies." *Journal of Consulting and Clinical Psychology* 63.5 (1995) 802–9.

Harris, Sam. "Free Will and "Free Will."" *SamHarris.org.* https://samharris.org/free-will-and-free-will/.

Haught, James. *2000 Years of Disbelief.* Amherst: Prometheus, 2006.

Headey, B., et al. "Authentic happiness theory supported by impact of religion on life satisfaction: A longitudinal analysis with data for Germany." *The Journal of Positive Psychology* 5 (2010) 73–82. doi:10.1080/17439760903435232.

Heelas, Paul. "The Infirmity Debate: On the Viability of New Age Spiritualities of Life." *Journal of Contemporary Religion*, 21.2 (2006) 223–40. doi: 10.1080/13537900600656066.

Heelas, Paul and Linda Woodhead, et al. *The Spiritual Revolution.* Malden: Blackwell, 2005.

Heritage Foundation. "Heritage Discusses Socialism with Jordan Peterson." *heritagefoundation.org.* https://www.myheritage.org/news/heritage-discusses-socialism-with-jordan-peterson/.

Hinojosa, Amanda S., et al. "A Review of Cognitive Dissonance Theory in Management Research: Opportunities for Further Development." *Journal of Management* 43.1 (January 2017) 170–99. https://doi.org/10.1177/0149206316668236.

Hutson, Matthew. "Why Liberals Aren't as Tolerant as They Think." *Politico*, May 9, 2017. https://www.politico.com/magazine/story/2017/05/09/why-liberals-arent-as-tolerant-as-they-think-215114.

Jones, Clay. *Why Does God Allow Evil? Compelling Answers for Life's Toughest Questions.* Eugene: Harvest House, 2001.

Jost, John T. and Aaron C. Kay. "Social Justice: History, Theory, and Research." *Handbook of Social Psychology.* Hoboken: John Wiley & Sons, 2010.

Keller, Timothy. *The Reason for God.* New York: Penguin Books, 2008.

Kengor, Paul. *The Devil and Karl Marx: Communism's Long March of Death, Deception, and Infiltration.* Ashland: TAN Books, 2020.

Keener, Craig. *The Bible Background Commentary.* Downers Grove: IVP, 2014.

Kirkpatrick, L. A. "An Attachment-Theory Approach to the Psychology of Religion." *The International Journal for the Psychology of Religion* 2 (1992) 3–28.

Koukl, Gregory. *Tactics.* Grand Rapids: Zondervan, 2018.

Bibliography

Knox, John S. *Sacro-Egoism: The Rise of Religious Individualism in the West.* Eugene: Wipf and Stock, 2016.

Kruger, Michael. *The Ten Commandments of Progressive Christianity.* Minneapolis: Cruciform, 2019.

Kunnen, E. S. "Are Conflicts the Motor in Identity Change?" *Identity* 6 (2006) 169–86.

Kushner, Harold S. *Nine Essential Things I've Learned About Life.* New York: Random House, 2015.

Lazarus, Clifford N. "The Depressing Truth about the Human Condition?" *psychologytoday.com.* https://www.psychologytoday.com/us/blog/think-well/201905/the-depressing-truth-about-the-human-condition.

Lee, Karen Adriana, and Peter Madsen Gubi. "Breaking up with Jesus: a phenomenological exploration of the experience of deconversion from an Evangelical Christian faith to Atheism." *Mental Health, Religion & Culture* 22.2 (2019) 171–84. doi: 10.1080/13674676.2019.1623767.

Lewis, C. S. *Spirits in Bondage.* Champaign: Project Gutenberg, 1990.

Lewis, Ralph. "Purpose, Meaning and Morality without God." *Psychology Today*, September 9, 2018. https://www.psychologytoday.com/us/blog/finding-purpose/201809/purpose-meaning-and-morality-without-god.

Ludemann, Gerd. *What Really Happened?* Louisville: Westminster, 1996.

Machen, J. Gresham. *Christianity and Liberalism.* Grand Rapids: Eerdmans, 1923.

Marriott, John. *A Recipe for Disaster: Four Ways Churches and Parents Prepare Individuals to Lose Their Faith and How They Can Instill a Faith That Endures.* Eugene: Wipf and Stock, 2018.

Marx, Karl. *The Communist Manifesto, part II, Proletarians and Communists.* http://www.marxists.org/archive/marx/works/1848/communist-manifesto/ch02.htm.

Milkie, Melissa A. "Changes in the Cultural Model of Father Involvement: Descriptions of Benefits to Fathers, Children, and Mothers in Parents' Magazine, 1926-2006." *Journal of Family Issues* 35.2 (January 2014) 223–53. https://doi.org/10.1177/0192513X12462566.

Mill, John Stuart. *On Liberty.* New York: Norton, 1975.

Mohammadi, Dara. "Finding Patient Zero." *The Pharmaceutical Journal* 294. 7845 (2015) 294. doi:10.1211/PJ.2015.20067543.

Muller, Rene. "Are We Hard-Wired for God?" *Psychiatric Times*, May 1, 2008. https://www.psychiatrictimes.com/view/neurotheology-are-we-hardwired-god.

Nielsen, Kai. "Why Should I Be Moral? Revisited." *American Philosophical Quarterly* 21.1 (1984) 90.

Nietzsche, Friedrich. *Thus Spoke Zarathustra.* London: Penguin, 2003.

O'Malley, Joseph. *Critique of Hegel's Philosophy of Right.* Cambridge: Cambridge Press, 1970.

Oppy, Graham. *Atheism: The Basics.* London: Routledge, 2019.

BIBLIOGRAPHY

Peterson, Jordan. "2016 Personality Lecture 05: Piaget Segueing into Jung." *Alpha Voice*, January 4, 2018. https://www.alphavoice.io/video/jordan-peterson/2016-personality-lecture-05-piaget-segueing-into-jung.

Pew Forum. "Putting Findings from the Religious Landscape Study into Context." *pewforum.org*. https://www.pewforum.org/2015/05/12/appendix-c-putting-findings-from-the-religious-landscape-study-into-context/.

———. *US Public Becoming Less Religious*. https://www.pewforum.org/2015/11/03/u-s-public-becoming-less-religious.

Pew Research. "The Countries With the 10 Largest Christian Populations." *pewresearch.org*. https://www.pewresearch.org/fact-tank/2019/04/01/the-countries-with-the-10-largest-christian-populations-and-the-10-largest-muslim-populations.

———. "In US, Decline of Christianity Continues at a Rapid Pace." https://www.pewforum.org/2019/10/17/in-u-s-decline-of-christianity-continues-at-rapid-pace/.

Phillips III, R. E. "A Re-examination of Religious Fundamentalism: Positive Implications for Coping." *Mental Health, Religion & Culture* 18 (2015) 299–311.

Pitts, F. H. "A Liberal Marxism? Mutual Care, Global Humanity and Minimum Utopia." *The Political Quarterly* 91 (2020) 235–42. doi:10.1111/1467-923X.12809.

Plantinga, Alvin. "Naturalism, Theism, Obligation and Supervenience." *Faith and Philosophy: Journal of the Society of Christian Philosophers* 27.3 (2010) 247–72. doi: 10.5840/faithphil201027328.

———. *Where the Conflict Really Lies: Science, Religion, & Naturalism*. Oxford University Press, 2011.

Ravenhill, Leonard. *Why Revival Tarries*. Bloomington: Bethany House, 1987.

Roche, Staks. "Atheism has a Suicide Problem." *Huffington Post*, December 8, 2017. https://www.huffpost.com/entry/atheism-has-a-suicide-problem_b_5a2a902ee4b022ec613b812b.

Ross, K. H. "Losing Faith in Fundamental Christianity: An Interpretative Phenomenological Analysis" (Unpublished master's thesis, University of Toronto, 2009). https://tspace.library.utoronto.ca/bitstream/1807/18123/11/Ross_Karen_H_200911_MA_thesis.pdf.

Showalter, Brandon. "US Christians Increasing Departing from Core Truths of Christian Worldview, Survey Finds." *Christian Post*, August 9, 2020. https://www.christianpost.com/news/us-christians-increasingly-departing-from-core-truths-of-christian-worldview-survey-finds.html.

Smith, Christian. *Soul Searching: The Religious and Spiritual Lives of the American Teenager*. Oxford: Oxford University Press, 2005.

Smith, Gregory. "America's Changing Religious Landscape." *Pew Research Center*.

Bibliography

Sowell, Thomas. "Blame the Welfare State, not Racism, for Poor Black's Problems." *Penn Live*, May 7, 2015. https://www.pennlive.com/opinion/2015/05/poor_blacks_looking_for_someon.html.

Spyropoulos, George. "A Portfolio of Academic, Therapeutic Practice and Research Work, Including a Grounded Theory Exploration of Deconversion From Religious Belief." https://epubs.surrey.ac.uk/846153/1/Final%20Portfolio%20Revised%20George_Spyropoulos.pdf.

Stark, Rodney, and Roger Finke. *Acts of Faith: Explaining the Human Side of Religion*. Berkeley: University of California Press, 2000.

Strayer, J. "The Dynamics of Emotions and Life Cycle Identity." *Identity: An International Journal of Theory and Research* 2 (2002) 47–79.

Streib, H., et al. "Deconversion: Qualitative and Quantitative Results from Cross-Cultural Research in Germany and the United States of America." *Vandenhoeck & Ruprecht* 5 (2011) 41.

Tarrants, Thomas A. "True Conversions and Wholehearted Commitment: Foundations of Discipleship." *CSlewisinstitue.org*. https://www.cslewisinstitute.org/True_Conversion_and_Wholehearted_Commitment_SinglePage%20.

Taunton, Larry Alex. "Listening to Young Atheists." *The Atlantic*, June 6, 2013. https://www.theatlantic.com/national/archive/2013/06/listening-to-young-atheists-lessons-for-a-stronger-christianity/276584/?utm_source=share&utm_campaign=share.

———. *The Grace Effect: How the Power of One Life Can Reverse the Corruption of Unbelief*. Nashville: Thomas Nelson, 2011.

Tillman, William M. "The Church's Response to Homosexuality: Biblical Models for the 21st Century." *Review & Expositor* 98.2 (May 2001) 243–60. https://doi.org/10.1177/003463730109800207.

Tolston, Art. "Akin, Mohler Dispute Claim of Liberal Drift." *Baptist Press*, August 1, 2019. https://www.baptistpress.com/resource-library/news/akin-mohler-dispute-claim-of-sbc-liberal-drift/.

Troeltsch, Ernst. *The Social Teaching of the Christian Churches*. Chicago: University of Chicago Press, 1981.

Van der Westhuizen, H. "'Who is Christ for Us Today?' Bonhoeffer's Question for the Church." *Acta Theologica* 37.2 (2017) 143-67.

Virgil, *The Aeneid of Virgil*. New York: Bantam Books, 1981.

Vitz, Paul C. *Psychology as Religion: The Cult of Self-Worship*. Carlisle: Paternoster, 2001.

Vohs, K.D. and J. W. Schooler. "The Value of Believing in Free Will: Encouraging a Belief in Determinism Increases Cheating." *Psychological Science* 19.1 (2008) 49–54. doi:10.1111/j.1467-9280.2008.02045.x.

Waite, L. J., and Lehrer, E. L. "The benefits from marriage and religion in the United States: A comparative analysis." *Population and Development Review* 29 (2003) 255–75. doi:10.1111/j.1728-4457.2003.00255.X

Warren, Rick. *The Purpose Driven Life*. Cedar Rapids: Zondervan, 2002.

Westcott, B. F. *The Gospel of the Resurrection*. London: Macmillan, 1879.

BIBLIOGRAPHY

White, James. *The Rise of the Nones: Understanding and Reaching the Religiously Unaffiliated.* Ada: Baker, 2014.

White, Tim. "To Black Lives Matter, No Lives Matter." *Objective Standard: A Journal of Culture & Politics* 15.3 (2020) 88–94.

Whitt, Kyle. Interview by the author. Teleconference (June 23, 2021).

Wiersby, Warren. *The Bible Exposition Commentary.* Colorado Springs: Cook, 1989.

Wright, N. T. "The New Unimproved Jesus." *Christianity Today,* September 13, 1993. https://www.christianitytoday.com/ct/1993/september-13/new-unimproved-jesus.html.

Zacharias, Ravi. *Cries of the Heart.* Grand Rapids: Zondervan, 1998.

Index

A

abandonment, 14, 22
abortion, 26, 68, 81
Abrahamic, 53
accomplish, 12, 68
accountability, 6-8, 35, 42-43, 103-104
accusation, 33, 43, 64, 92
action, xii, 2, 7, 39, 41, 62, 68, 93
activism, 73, 80-81
Adam, 25, 111
Adler, 2, 111
adult, 79, 81, 88, 93, 111
affirmation, 2, 19
agenda, 9, 17, 99
agnosticism, 20, 24, 102
analogy, 67
analysis, 14, 21-22, 38, 47, 77, 102, 111, 113, 115-116
antithesis, 15, 24, 66, 81, 83
apologetic, vii, x, xiii, 3, 5, 12-13, 17, 20-23, 31-32, 43, 48-49, 52, 54-56, 63-65, 71-72, 91-92, 105, 111
Apologist, 12-13, 16, 18, 22, 29, 48-49, 52, 55-56, 62-63, 70, 77, 105
apostasy, ix-x, 1, 24, 32, 52, 72, 101, 111

apostate, 1-2, 13, 19, 23-24, 26, 29-30, 33-34, 40, 42-43, 48, 52, 59, 73, 83, 86, 90, 93, 104, 111-112
apostle, xv, 19, 22, 27, 90, 94
appearance, 42, 44, 57-58, 88
Aquinas, 22, 68, 112
archetypes, 24
Aristotle, 68
Ascol, 10
atheism, 1, 7, 12-14, 20-21, 24-25, 34-35, 41, 44-45, 51, 58, 61-62, 64-65, 69, 76, 78, 80-83, 102, 104, 108-109, 112-115
atheist, 6, 14-15, 19, 22, 24-25, 30, 32-35, 38-40,
(atheist continued)
44-46, 48-51, 58, 61-63, 66-71, 73, 77-82, 85, 89, 92-93, 102-103, 108-109, 112-113, 116
Auschwitz, 74
authoritative, 4, 29, 31, 55, 84

B

Bahnsen, 55-56, 111
Baptist, xv, 37, 97, 116

Index

Barr, 36, 111
believer, x–xi, xiii, 1, 7–8, 12–13, 16, 18, 32, 34, 38, 41, 46, 54–55, 62, 65, 84, 96, 101
beneficial, 12, 15
benevolence, 93
Berlinski, 111
Bible, xvi, 4, 6–7, 24, 26, 29–31, 33, 35, 37, 39–41, 56, 59, 61, 65, 69, 84, 88–89, 92, 95, 108, 113, 117
Biblical, 6, 12, 15, 17–19, 22–26, 31–32, 35, 39–40, 50, 52, 54, 59–60, 66, 69–70, 72, 74–75, 79, 84, 87, 97–99, 105, 108, 116
Bonhoeffer, 18, 116
Boomers, 13, 18
Bromley, 24, 111
Bukowski, 73
Bush, 9, 111

C

Calvinist, 55
Cammaerts, 16, 73, 112
capitalism, 17, 27
charitable, 93
Chesterton, 22, 112
Christianity, ix, xii, 1–3, 5–7, 11–12, 14–19, 21–23, 25, 29, 34, 38, 41, 43, 52–54, 56, 58–60, 63–65, 72, 79, 81, 86, 88–90, 93, 98, 101–102, 105, 108, 114–117
churched, xi, 85, 87
clergy, 43
clinical, 46, 77, 113
cognition, 25–26, 50
Cognitive, 14, 25–26, 28–29, 31, 47–48, 50, 56, 87, 89, 104, 113
Colossians, xvi, 60, 84
commandments, 39, 94, 112, 114

commitment, ix, 1, 8, 15, 18–19, 25–26, 32, 43, 48, 59–60, 65, 67, 85, 93, 99, 116
Communism, 9, 11, 27, 113
Communist, 9, 11, 82, 85, 114
compassion, 79, 93
confessions, 75, 78, 111
congregant, 19, 37, 53, 64, 72, 94
congregation, xi, 79, 91
constitution, 27, 36
contradiction, 15, 29, 44, 51, 79
contradictory, 25, 30, 75, 77, 79
conviction, ix, 2, 6, 24, 37, 44, 57, 73
Copan, 112
Corinthians, 58, 60, 66, 95, 101
Cosmology, 31, 41
counseling, 111–112
covenant, 26, 53
creation, 33–34, 40, 59–60, 69, 76, 102–103, 105
Creator, ix, 1–2, 12, 23, 30, 32, 34, 53, 57, 61, 69, 77
creature, 6, 9, 67–68, 75, 82, 103
crucifixion, 77
cult, 76, 116

D

Darwinian, 25, 50, 65, 68–69, 74, 77, 112
deconstruction, iii–iv, xiii
deconversion, ix–x, xii–xiii, 1–2, 6, 9–10, 14–15, 17, 19–21, 23, 25, 28–29, 31, 36–37, 41–43, 49, 52, 56, 64, 71, 89–92, 104, 107–109, 112, 114, 116
deconvert, vii, 7, 13–14, 17, 19–21, 23, 25, 32, 37, 40, 43, 47, 53–54, 88–89, 93, 102–104
deconverted, i, iii–iv, xiii, 1, 6, 8, 13, 15, 17–18, 21–22, 25, 43, 47–49, 64, 71–73, 85, 92, 105

Index

Deity, 23, 37–38, 40, 73–74, 78, 82, 102, 105
delusion, 23, 38, 111–112
Descartes, 68
Deuteronomy, 26, 29, 62
diagnosis, vii, 37, 43, 79
dichotomy, 35, 60, 77, 81
directive, 31, 92, 95
disbelief, 2, 20, 73, 80, 113
discernment, 12, 99
disciple, x, 43, 57, 71, 94, 100
discipleship, x, 17, 19, 64, 71–72, 91–92, 116
disease, 13, 34, 55
disorder, 37, 41, 51
dispair, 33
dissonance, 25–26, 29, 31, 47–48, 87, 89, 104, 113
divine, 4, 30, 39, 64, 77–78, 101
divinity, 79, 95
DNA, 44, 49–50, 66
doctrine, 7, 17, 19, 23, 26, 28–29, 31, 37, 52, 71, 77–78, 81, 84, 90, 99
dogma, 3, 19, 108
Dueck, 33, 112
Duignan, 8, 112
duty, 13, 39, 45, 58, 69

E

Eden, 33, 50, 112
Egoism, 4–5, 14, 17, 87, 91, 114
Ehrman, 57, 112
Ellens, 52–53, 112
enemy, 48, 60, 83, 91, 99
environmental, 8
Ephesians, 29, 52, 89, 95
Epicurean, 38
epidemic, vii, ix, 4
epistemology, 13
eschatological, 58
eternal, xii, 19, 34, 42, 58, 63

ethic, 12, 16, 39, 66, 70, 81, 88, 90, 111
ethos, 3
Evangelical, 24, 57, 90, 93, 111, 114
evangelist, 95–96
evidentialist, 13, 85
evolution, 6, 14, 50, 65, 77, 81, 87
Existentialism, 65–66
existentialist, 66, 68
Exodus, 26, 29
experientialism, 13, 18

F

failure, 11, 28, 33, 40, 43, 65, 69
faith, ix–x, xii–xiii, 1–2, 5, 7, 11, 13–14, 16, 18–19, 21, 23, 26, 30, 39–40, 43, 52, 55, 59, 64–65, 69, 72–73, 77–78, 82–83, 87, 90, 92, 95, 101–102, 105, 107–108, 112, 114–116
fellowship, 14, 71
feminism, 10
fetus, 68
Frankl, 74–75, 113
freedom, 30, 35, 41–42, 44, 48, 77, 80, 83, 90
freethinkers, 44
freethinking, 49, 82
fulfillment, 41, 54, 60, 76
Fundamentalism, 90–91, 111, 115
fundamentalist, 15, 84, 89, 111

G

Galatians, 62, 77, 94–95
geared, xii
generation, 48, 61, 76, 96, 99
Genesis, 27, 50, 53, 95
Godhead, 2, 75
godless, 10, 68, 78, 97
Gospel, 6, 11–12, 24, 43, 47–48, 62, 72–73, 77, 94–100, 116

Index

Gottfried, 70
guilt, 6, 53

H

Hackney, 77, 113
Haidt, 88, 113
happiness, 76–77, 113
heaven, 18, 39–40, 63
Hebrews, 95–96
hedonism, 91
Heelas, 5, 113
hegemony, 112
hiddenness, 37–39
hierarchy, 15, 35, 40, 67, 73, 75, 87, 91, 105
Hinojosa, 25–26, 113
historical, 19, 27, 38, 43, 52, 57–58, 79, 85, 87, 101
Hitchens, 63
Hoboken, 113
homosexuality, 27, 31, 79, 84, 116
http, 111–117
humanism, 34, 38, 49, 51, 76
humanity, ix, 2, 6, 9, 31, 33–35, 40, 44–47, 53–54, 60, 65–66, 70, 72, 74, 77–78, 80–83, 85, 89, 95–96, 102–104, 112, 115

I

ideological, 1, 3, 5, 8, 10, 13–18, 21, 23, 31, 34–37, 48, 54, 65, 71, 85–88, 90, 97, 102
ideology, ix, 1–2, 8–15, 22–23, 28, 34–35, 37–38, 43, 45, 52, 61, 77–79, 81, 83–85, 87, 90, 97–99, 102, 107
immoralism, 66
Individualism, 4, 114
indoctrination, 30, 32
inerrancy, 37, 98, 108
inerrant, 31

injustice, 33, 98–99
institution, 8–10, 17, 19, 32, 79, 97
intellectual, 8, 10, 14–15, 17–18, 21, 25, 32, 34–35, 38, 47, 51–52, 56, 64, 69–70, 72, 75, 78, 80, 87, 89, 91, 99, 101–103
interpretation, 23–24, 26, 29, 46, 55, 81–82, 84, 98, 101, 105
intersectionality, 10, 98
Irenaeus, 68
Isaac, 112
Isaiah, 69
Islam, 101

J

judgement, 6, 47, 69, 75, 88
Jung, 47, 115
justice, 9–11, 27, 50, 60, 66–67, 78–79, 84, 94, 97–99, 113
justification, 13, 24

K

Kengor, 10–11, 113
kingdom, 18, 95
Koukl, 103, 113
Kruger, 114
Kushner, 55, 114

L

Lazarus, 66, 114
leadership, 43, 48, 64, 92, 99
leftist, 8–9, 17, 27, 48, 81, 84–85, 87, 96
Leibniz, 70
liberalism, 7, 12, 37, 59, 114
logos, 47, 85
Ludemann, 57, 114
Luke, 6, 18, 39, 91–92

Index

M

Machen, 7, 12, 59, 114
Maidanek, 74
marriage, vi, 18, 26, 77, 81, 84, 95, 116
Marx, 9–11, 82, 113–114
Marxism, ix, 10–11, 27–28, 54, 97, 99, 115
materialism, 74, 91
millennials, 13, 18
ministry, xi, xiii, 55, 74, 79, 95
miracle, 4, 29, 62
Mohler, 11, 116
monotheism, 44, 67, 78, 82–83
morality, ix, 1, 6, 8–9, 12, 16–19, 22–23, 31, 34–36, 42, 44, 50, 53–54, 57–59, 66–69, 77, 79, 84, 86, 88, 91, 102–105, 108, 114

N

narcissism, 76
Naturalism, 4, 6, 12–13, 21, 34, 49–50, 115
Nazareth, 112
neurotheology, 114
Nietzsche, 66, 82, 85, 111, 114
nihilism, 74
nonbeliever, 64, 73

O

oppression, 9, 27, 83–84
oppressor, 10, 27, 97, 99
Oppy, 35, 114
organization, 24, 26, 30, 40, 71, 80, 92–93
outreach, 40, 92–93

P

pastor, xii, xv, 10, 37, 76, 94, 96
Paul, xv, 10, 19, 22, 57, 60, 74–75, 77, 89–90, 94–95, 111–113, 116
perception, 5, 50, 74, 86–87, 93
Peterson, 46–47, 84–85, 113, 115
Pew, x, 2–3, 17, 19, 22, 48–49, 61, 91, 104, 115
pharisee, 53–54
phenomenological, 111, 114–115
Philippians, 54, 95–96
philosopher, 2, 36, 44, 51, 55, 62, 66, 70, 75, 115
philosophy, ix, 1, 8–9, 15, 19, 25, 30, 45, 49, 51, 59, 66, 72, 83, 112, 114–115
Piaget, 47, 115
Plantinga, 50, 70, 115
Plato, 68
pluralism, 60
posited, 16, 47, 66
positivism, 45
postmodernism, ix, 8, 16, 75, 112
prayer, 18, 29–30, 38, 72, 96–97
presupposition, 7, 13–14, 22, 29, 31–32, 43, 45, 48, 52, 54–55, 59, 64, 66, 92
presuppositional, 13, 32, 52–53, 55–56, 63, 86–87, 92, 111
progressive, 11–12, 68, 114
proof, 13, 21, 29, 31–34, 44, 54, 65, 80, 92, 97, 102
propaganda, 12, 16, 19, 23, 27–28, 33, 40, 48, 50, 62, 72, 81, 88, 92, 96, 98, 100
prophecy, 23, 74, 108
prophet, 16, 57, 73, 112
protestant, 24, 91, 111
Proverbs, 66, 95
Psalm, 62, 76, 89, 95
psychologist, 14, 46–47, 51–52, 68, 75–76, 88–89, 91, 112

Index

Psychology, xiii, xv, 15, 68, 75–77, 89, 113–114, 116

R

racial, 10, 98–99
racism, 28, 84, 116
rationalize, 36, 52, 66, 84
Ravenhill, 48, 96, 115
reality, 3, 6, 12–14, 19, 27, 29, 33–35, 48, 50, 55–58, 66, 76–77, 83, 87–88, 90, 105
reconcile, 14, 37, 41, 84
redemption, 6–7, 9, 39–40, 47, 52–54, 65, 67, 78, 81–82, 90, 93, 98, 101
rejection, x, 2, 7, 16, 19, 26, 32, 44, 56, 62, 64, 71–72, 79, 88–89, 98, 105
relationship, ix, xi, 1, 4, 24–25, 53, 58, 65, 72, 103–104
relativism, 8, 60, 83, 85
religiosity, 4–5, 40, 52, 77, 113
responsibility, 28, 83, 104
resurrection, 23, 29, 37, 43, 57–59, 62, 72, 92, 95, 105, 108, 116
revival, 48, 96, 115
righteousness, 27, 40–42, 78, 89
Routledge, 114

S

sacro, 4–5, 14, 17, 87, 114
salvation, 6, 19, 39–40, 95
Samuel, 62
sanctification, 6
sanctity, 84, 88, 95
Satan, 76, 91, 104
Savior, xv, 65, 92
SBC, 10, 97–98, 116
scholar, 5, 39, 55, 57–58, 70, 84
scholarly, xv, 19, 45, 102

scientific, 8, 12, 30, 35, 45, 49, 52, 77, 81, 103, 113
scientism, 51, 74, 76, 81
Scripture, 18–19, 31, 38, 50, 54–56, 60, 66, 69, 84, 86, 94–95, 97, 105
secular, 8–9, 13, 34–35, 38, 44, 46, 49, 51, 53–54, 66–68, 76, 78, 80, 88, 93
Seeker, 14, 21, 48, 71, 85–86, 89, 94
sexuality, 30, 99, 104
Showalter, 19, 115
sinner, 48, 56
skeptic, 32, 34, 48–49
skepticism, 8, 45
slavery, 24, 29
Socialism, 10, 27, 60, 85, 113
Socrates, 61
soul, 9, 12, 38, 50, 53, 58, 60, 62, 75, 80, 92, 96, 113, 115
Sowell, 28, 116
spiritual, ix, 2, 4–5, 7, 12–13, 17–18, 22, 31, 39, 48–49, 52–53, 56–57, 60, 64, 71–72, 79, 91–92, 96–97, 99–100, 105, 113, 115
spirituality, 5, 25, 38, 53, 78, 113
Spyropoulos, 28–29, 116
strawman, 24, 59, 65, 69
Streib, 31, 116
Strobel, 63
subjectivism, 8
substantiation, 44, 85
suicide, 37, 45–46, 112, 115
supererogatory, 39–40
supernatural, 3–4, 7, 32–33, 49, 58, 64, 96
symptom, 75, 98

T

Taunton, 63, 116
tension, 5, 7, 16, 26, 28, 88
testament, 16, 57–59, 94

INDEX

theism, 24, 31, 35, 45, 50, 61, 64, 79, 102, 108, 115
theist, 2, 12, 24, 29–30, 34, 38, 46, 48, 51, 57, 61, 66, 75, 80, 108
theodicy, 49, 112
theologian, 18, 50, 52, 57, 72, 75, 87
theological, vii, 1–2, 6–7, 13, 15–17, 21–22, 31–32, 34, 43, 47, 52, 54, 61, 68, 72, 86–88, 105, 112
theology, xv, 6, 15, 17, 64, 112
theory, 5, 10, 15, 25–26, 45, 65, 69, 74, 77, 81, 97, 112–113, 116
therapeutic, 29, 38, 116
threat, 79, 90, 98, 101
Timothy, 29, 48, 74, 94–95, 113
tradition, 9, 11, 26, 40, 57, 76
transcendence, 25, 34
transcendent, 1–2, 4, 7, 18, 25, 32–33, 36–37, 41, 45, 52, 57–59, 61, 64, 67, 69, 74, 77–78, 87–88, 92, 101
transformation, 65, 111
Troeltsch, 116
truth, vi, xiii, 6–8, 16, 18–19, 23, 31–32, 34, 36, 40, 44, 48, 50, 53, 58–59, 61–62, 66–67, 69, 73–75, 77–78, 84–85, 88, 90, 92, 94–96, 100–105, 114–115

U

unbelief, 24, 29, 54, 83, 116
unbeliever, 34, 38, 56, 97
Unchurched, 85–86

Universalist, 78–79, 90
universe, 1–2, 12, 23, 33, 49, 68, 78, 87, 103
unobservable, 34, 64
utilitarian, 11, 51, 72

V

Vandenhoeck, 116
virtue, 36, 83, 112

W

warfare, 12, 22, 27, 59, 71, 92, 96–97, 99
Westcott, 72, 116
Westhuizen, 18, 116
Whitson, xv
Whitt, 97–99, 117
Wiersby, 39–40, 117
Wiley, 113
Woodhead, 5, 113
worldview, ix, 1–2, 6, 8, 10, 12–16, 18, 22–24, 30, 32, 35, 37–38, 41, 44–46, 48, 51, 54, 58, 64, 66, 68–69, 79, 83–85, 87, 92, 97, 101–102, 115
worship, 2, 30, 32, 34, 49, 56, 60, 73–74, 77, 82, 103, 116

Z

Zarathustra, 82, 114

www.ingramcontent.com/pod-product-compliance
Lightning Source LLC
Chambersburg PA
CBHW072155160426
43197CB00012B/2394